Jordan Elliott 7/2/2010

W9-AVB-374

QUEER QUOTES

QUEER QUOTES

On Coming Out and Culture, Love and Lust,
Politics and Pride, and Much More

Edited by **TERESA THEOPHANO**

BEACON
150   *Beacon Press, Boston*

BEACON PRESS
25 Beacon Street
Boston, Massachusetts 02108-2892
www.beacon.org

Beacon Press books
are published under the auspices of
the Unitarian Universalist Association of
Congregations.

© 2004 by Teresa Theophano

All rights reserved
Printed in the United States of America

08 07 06 05 04 8 7 6 5 4 3 2 1

This book is printed on acid-free paper that
meets the uncoated paper ANSI/NISO specifica-
tions for permanence as revised in 1992.

Text design by George Restrepo

Library of Congress Cataloging-in-Publication
Data

Queer quotes : on coming out and culture, love
and lust, politics and pride, and much more /
[compiled by] Teresa Theophano.
        p. cm.
Includes index.
ISBN 0-8070-7906-5 (alk. paper)
1. Gays—Quotations. 2. Homosexuality—
Quotations, maxims, etc. I. Theophano, Teresa.
PN6084.G35Q45 2004
306.76'6—dc22   2004004490

Author's note: In the Biographies section,
p. 139, I have provided birth and death dates
for persons quoted in the book whenever they
were available.

FOR SHANNON

TABLE OF CONTENTS

INTRODUCTION

I set out to compile this book knowing there had been other similar tomes in the past. Why did I think this one would be so different?

Well, there were several reasons. First, it's the year 2004, and things have changed greatly since the last book of quotes by, for, and about the queer community was published. For one, we're making huge strides in progress. While I was working on this book, the State Supreme Court of Massachusetts had just ruled in favor of gay marriage—already legalized in Ontario, Canada earlier that year—and the Texas sodomy law had recently been overridden. Civil unions between same-sex partners had been legalized in Vermont. Democratic presidential candidates who actually seemed serious about gay rights in their platforms had emerged. And while we still have a long way to go, my optimism has been soaring because, in this rocky and conservative political and economic time, we've seen some major triumphs for GLBTQ people—and some interesting quips to go alongside them.

Another thing that has changed as of late is the increased visibility of transgender folk—both within the queer community and in the larger society. Transgender, for those who don't already know, is an umbrella term that includes all types of people—transsexuals, drag kings, drag queens, two-spirits, bi-gendered folk—who fall between the cracks of the traditional binary gender system. Many would argue that the social construction of a gender binary is just as oppressive and damaging as homophobia. To my dismay, much queer literature published in the past has marginalized or ignored altogether this segment of humanity. I wanted to put together a book that would include the too-often-overlooked commentary and experience of transgender people.

Researching *Queer Quotes* was a real learning experience and an entertaining one at the same time, and for that I'm grateful. By scouring media sources queer, straight, mainstream, and cutting-edge—including piles upon piles of gay magazines, several volumes from my personal library of queer fiction and nonfiction, zines both old and new, almanacs, anthologies, and the Internet—I came across a wealth of information and a poignant reflection of what it means to be GLBTQ today. I have done my best to include quotes from various ethnic, socioeconomic, and cultural groups within the GLBTQ communities, and have represented verbatim quotes as closely as possible.

Naturally, I don't agree with every comment featured in this book, but I think it's important to include a wide spectrum of opinions and theories on our community. I hope you will find food for thought as well as a laugh in the pages of this book; whether read section by section or one quote at a time, *Queer Quotes* is an example of just how rich our culture, history, and politics really are.

To that end, I purposely avoided including sound bites from homophobes. We already know what the Trent Lotts, Jerry Falwells, and Fred Phelps of the world think of GLBT issues. We experience homophobia and heterosexism firsthand just about every day of our lives. Why offer them any more attention than they've already been given? Let's celebrate what we have, what we're striving toward, and who we are. Let's be utterly, joyously, and quotably queer!

"As everyone knows, a fag is a homosexual gentleman who has just left the room." —Truman Capote

"Above all, the lesbian and gay community is recognized as a community, one that is often angry and militant, generally well disciplined, always concerned." —Edmund White

"Anyone who thinks that love needs to be cured has not experienced enough of it in their own lives." —Joan Garry

"It is better to be hated for what one is than be loved for what one is not." —Andre Gide

"You're neither unnatural, nor abominable, nor mad; you're as much a part of what people call nature as anyone else; only you're unexplained as yet—you've not got your niche in creation." —Radclyffe Hall in The Well of Loneliness (1928)

"There is probably no sensitive heterosexual alive who is not preoccupied with his latent homosexuality." —Norman Mailer

"In itself, homosexuality is as limiting as heterosexuality: the idea should be to be capable of loving a woman or a man; either, a human being, without feeling fear, restraint, or obligation."

—Simone de Beauvoir

"The black community is only now beginning to realize the extent of bisexuality and homosexuality within our community, but it's here. It's been here for a long time and it's going to continue to be here. We might as well acknowledge it and move on." —Marlon Riggs

"It's no wonder we know how to dress; we've spent centuries in closets." —Isaac Mizrahi

"If I went onstage in a business suit, they would think I was crazy. It's like putting Marlene Dietrich in a housedress."

—Liberace

"Black men loving Black men is a call to action, an acknowledgement of responsibility. We take care of our own kind when the night grows cold and silent. These days the nights are cold-blooded and the silence echoes with complicity."

—Joseph Beam

"Remember, to hate, to be violent, is demeaning. It means you're afraid of the other side of the coin—to love and be loved." —James Baldwin

"The fear of homosexuality is found in movies more often than homosexuality itself." —Vito Russo

"They never asked me until Serial Mom and then every reviewer asked me if I was gay. . . . What are they, blind? Do they think a straight man could have made those movies?"

—John Waters

"Gay liberation should not be a license to be a perpetual adolescent. If you deny yourself commitment then what can you do with your life?" —Harvey Fierstein

"*Homosexuality strikes at the heart of the organization of Western culture and societies. Because homosexuality, by its nature, is nonreproductive, it posits a sexuality that is justified by pleasure alone.*" —Michael Bronski

"*There's a big difference between tolerance and approval, and I have no right to expect or demand the latter from anyone.*"
—Norah Vincent

"*I don't look like anyone else on TV. I'm bald, and I have a beard; how often do you see that? And I think they like my theatrics— my devilish sense of fun.*" —Christopher Lowell

"*The division of the population into 'gay' and 'straight' is a Western First World notion that has not been around very long and will not persist into the future.*" —Rex Wockner

"*When you look at the level of different experiences we've had, and how that crazy filter we all share of coming out and having to find our own ways in this world has made us different peo-*

ple, it's really exciting. I feel very proud of being gay. I still feel like I'm part of the coolest club." —Sarah Petitt

"I don't want to be tolerated. That offends my love of life and of liberty." —Jean Cocteau

"If I believe in anything, rather than God, it's that I am part of something that goes back to Antigone and that whatever speaks the truth of our hearts can only make us stronger. We must be the last generation to live in silence." —Paul Monette

"As Socrates said, 'The untelevised life is not worth living.'"
—Gore Vidal

"I truly believe that bisexuality is the natural human condition."
—Lillian Faderman

"I attribute a large part of the ignorance in schools to homophobia, because kids are fearful of being perceived as being different, even when they aren't actually gay. Teachers have to *challenge bigotry in all its forms, because bigotry is a way of making people act in ways that are not who they are."*

—Kevin Jennings

"If I had to choose one particular thing I've done and put it at the pinnacle of all of which I'm proud, it would be 'Gay is Good.' It encapsulates, in a way that has been taken up by others, everything that I stand for and have worked for."

—Frank Kameny, on the phrase he coined in the 1960s

NAMING OURSELVES

"*A person's sexuality is so much more than one word 'gay.' No one refers to anyone as just 'hetero' because that doesn't say anything. Sexual identity is broader than a label.*"

—Gus Van Sant

"*I really like the word* queer *because it embraces a genuine sense of the different, the otherness, most of us felt growing up. And being gay—being queer—is so much more than just being homosexual. It's a distinct sense of being outside something, looking in.*" —Jenifer Levin

"*My ultimate objective is to help create a society where people no longer define themselves as gay, straight and bisexual. When all three orientations are deemed equally valid and all intolerance is eradicated, there will be no need to differentiate between people of different sexualities.*"

—Peter Tatchell

"*I consider myself bisexual, and my philosophy is, everyone innately is. . . . I haven't explored it to the degree that I'd like to, but I'll tell you, I'm open to it. And I don't have any problem saying that."* —Megan Mullally

"Accept no one's definition of your life, but define yourself."
—Harvey Fierstein

"I don't want to have some adjective preceding my name for the rest of my life, whatever it may be, however people want to pigeonhole me. Is that mildly vague enough?"
—Rosie O'Donnell

"I am not just a lesbian. I am not just a poet. I am not just a mother. Honor the complexity of your vision and yourselves."
—Audre Lorde

"I'm still not crazy about the word gay, because I think it conjures up a certain stereotypical image. I like the idea that so many younger people today are using other terms, like queer. I took some heat from a lot of people when I did an interview and said I don't like to use the word gay." —Michael Feinstein

"I'll take 'bisexual' if I have to have a label. . . . I acknowledge that I respond erotically and romantically to a variety of people, including some men and some women." —David Bianco

"I've had long-term sexual relationships with both men and women. If that classifies me as bisexual, then I'm bisexual."
—Sandra Bernhard

"I want society to cease viewing gays as defined solely by our sexuality, and at the same time I want the freedom to be as unabashedly sexual as I wish." —Vito Russo

"How long will it be before [gay] isn't the adjective, the descriptive term? . . . How about human being, mother, grandmother? How about just my name?" —Margarethe Cammermeyer

"I hate it when gay men are referred to as boys. And never more than when I hear grown gay men refer to themselves that way."
—Richard Gollance

"I am not especially defined by my sex life, nor complete without it." —Paula Gunn Allen

"I, Mabel Hampton, have been a lesbian all my life, for eighty-two years, and I am proud of myself and my people. I would like all my people to be free in this country and all over the world, my gay people and my black people." —Mabel Hampton, in her address at the 1984 New York City pride rally

"If there were no fear of, or discrimination against, lesbians and gays, maybe just 'a person' would do. But our social instinct is to name, to define, even when those appellations become confining or negative." —Jewelle Gomez

"I don't believe there is such a thing as gay or straight. I think the only thing that exists is sexuality. . . . To me, a truly evolved person is bisexual, or at least open to the possibility of being bisexual." —Boy George

"I don't care how anyone identifies me as long as I can do my work." —Lily Tomlin

"The 'love that dare not speak its name' in this century is ... that deep, spiritual affection that is as pure as it is perfect. It is beautiful, it is fine, it is the noblest form of affection. There is nothing unnatural about it." —Oscar Wilde

"I could love anything on earth that appeared to wish it."

—Lord Byron

"I have waited years for you who wants to flaunt me on her arm, my face radiant with desire, as if I'd put my face deep into a lily, heavy with pollen, and raised it to you, smeared and smelly with butter yellow, sated but not yet satisfied."

—Minnie Bruce Pratt

"When you're in love you never really know whether your elation comes from the qualities of the one you love, or if it attributes them to her; whether the light which surrounds her like a halo comes from you, from her, or from the meeting of your sparks."

—Natalie Clifford Barney

"I'm now clear in my mind that I do love you. If you won't come back or let me join you, you're committing a crime."

—Arthur Rimbaud, to Paul Verlaine

"We must declare ourselves, become known; allow the world to discover this subterranean life of ours which connects kings and farm boys, artists and clerks. Let them see that the important thing is not the object of love, but the emotion itself."

—Gore Vidal

"Love—romantic love or passion—seems to consist of nothing but perspective. . . . Love equals recognition. The lover is the only one who recognizes his beloved—which is why friends can never see what he sees in him." —Michael Denneny

"You must know, dear, how I long for you all the time and especially during the last three weeks. There is reason in the habit of married folks keeping together." —Jane Addams, to her partner, Mary Rozet Smith

"There's this illusion that homosexuals have sex and heterosexuals fall in love. That's completely untrue. Everybody wants to be loved." —Boy George

"How idiotic people are when they are in love. What an age-old devastating disease!" —Noel Coward

"Hick darling, . . . I couldn't say 'je t'aime et je t'adore' as I longed to do, but always remember I am saying it, that I go to sleep thinking of you."

—Eleanor Roosevelt, in a letter to Lorena Hickok

"One word frees us of all the weight and pain of life: that word is love." —Sophocles

"Gay marriage should be legal if just to raise the standard of dancing at receptions." —Liz Langley

"We declare that barring an individual from the protections, benefits and obligations of civil marriage solely because that person would marry a person of the same sex violates the Massachusetts constitution." —*Chief Justice Margaret Marshall, in her 2003 ruling in favor of gay marriage in the state of Massachusetts*

"Our [wedding] page is a community bulletin board about the important milestones in people's lives . . . I felt uncomfortable saying no." —*Charles Broadwell, on the* New York Times' *decision to run same-sex union announcements*

"Marriage is the premier issue of our community, the premier issue that would make all the difference for us in American culture." —*Rev. Troy Perry*

"I believe in exchanging bodily fluids, not wedding rings."
—*Scott O'Hara*

"The most successful marriages, gay or straight, even if they begin in romantic love, often become friendships. It's the ones that become the friendships that last." —*Andrew Sullivan*

"This decision puts wind in our sails, though our work clearly isn't over. Canada has now shown us we can win."

—Evan Wolfson, on the legalizing of gay marriage in Ontario

"What are you trying to protect heterosexual marriages from? There isn't a limited amount of love in Iowa. It isn't a non-renewable resource." —Rep. Ed Fallon

"One thousand forty-nine. That is the number of federal statutes that provide benefits, rights, and privileges to individuals who have the legal right to marry. I am at the end of my patience with gays who say they're not interested in obtaining the right to legally marry." —Larry Kramer

"The push for [gay] marriage is not an isolated phenomenon but signals hostility to sexual liberation. I wonder if we will all one day look back from another world and think about what gay life was like before the freedom from marriage was extinguished—in the same way that some look at (and remember) what life was like before AIDS." —Bill Dobbs

"In late December, our [Vermont] state Supreme Court ruled that same-sex couples are legally entitled to the same benefits and protections as married heterosexuals. And despite the fact that I'm a big, tough, out lesbian who doesn't need a court ruling to know that my relationship counts, even despite the fact that I like living in sin—I felt really, well, validated."

—Alison Bechdel

"I'm the longest-married woman in my family. I guess it was serious when we put them rings on. I put one in her left nipple and she put one in my pussy and ever since then we felt like we owned a piece of each other." —Dorothy Allison

"Marriage creates visibility. When we are banned from marrying, we are kept from doing publicly the ordinary and rational things that people do anyway—marry, settle down, get jobs, and live like everyone else." —Barbara Grier

THE ARTS

"My contribution to the world is my ability to draw. I will draw as much as I can for as many people as I can for as long as I can."
—Keith Haring

"I'm very proud that I represent the possibility for black gay men to write and create, that the possibility does exist, that you may even be able to do it full-time." —Essex Hemphill

"If God dislikes gays so much, how come he picked Michelangelo, a known homosexual, to paint the Sistine Chapel while assigning Anita [Bryant] to go on television and push orange juice?" —Mike Royko

"I still question the mainstream's ability to consistently find the cutting edge of gay and lesbian literature." —Felice Picano

"If you want to know all about Andy Warhol, just look at the surface of my paintings and films and me, and there I am. There's nothing behind it." —Andy Warhol

"The oppositions of race collide inside me, [and] my writing is always an attempt at reconciliation." —Cherrie Moraga

"The best thing about being a gay artist is you get to meet other gay artists and go hang out." —Gus Van Sant

"I am an actor. Of course I can play a heterosexual!"
—Sir John Gielgud

"When I write I don't do anything except smoke pot, eat, drink and write. I become this completely hedonistic, bohemian, out-of-control, raging, abusive writer." —k. d. lang

"When one is a Native lesbian, the desire to connect all becomes an urgent longing. Faced with homophobia from our own communities, faced with racism and homophobia from the outsiders who hold semblances of power over us, we feel that desire to connect in a primal way."
—Beth Brant, on her need to write

"Sensuality is one of the few presents nature has given us. It's a present we must celebrate. But here [in the U.S.], when a film explores that, it makes people nervous." —Pedro Almodovar

"If I'd taken up with a gospel band or rock and roll, I'd make a whole lot more sense to my family. But to write books. . . . I'd come home with books and they'd stare at me like I was crazy. That was the thing most queer about me." —Dorothy Allison

"I write about things that are going on in the lives of my friends: child abuse, AIDS, contaminated water that got into their system and gave them cancer. . . . The trick for the song-writer—for me—is to take these issues that are too painful to hear about and put them in a context so that you can listen."

—Holly Near

"There must be an agenda—every gay politician, spokeswoman and militant has shouted at me for not following it. . . . Right now, I'd love to see it, this set of rules . . . dictating what, how and why a gay writer must write." —Russell Davies

"I just make films about how I see the world. . . . I wanted to address the question of sexuality directly in a mainstream Hollywood film. But I've been around long enough to know that isn't a very easy thing to do." —John Schlesinger

"Writing is like working out with weights to me. If I lose one day I'm disturbed and everything is wobbly." —John Rechy

"Art . . . should be something that liberates the soul, provokes the imagination, and encourages people to go further."
—Keith Haring

"Hothead is basically a cartoon character who acted like I did when I was drunk." —Dianne DiMassa, on her infamous lesbian comic-book protagonist Hothead Paisan

"The creator of the new composition in arts is an outlaw until he is a classic. . . . For a very long time everybody refuses and then almost without a pause almost everybody accepts."
—Gertrude Stein

"I get really mad at bands who say they don't want to be pigeon-holed as a queer band. I have never been so proud to be [in] a queer band." —Beth Ditto of The Gossip

"There's a 'pyramid' scene that often happens in the art world. If you look at a performance place, you'll see they produce mostly white men (generally straight or closeted), one or two African-Americans, one or two lesbians (or one lesbian and one gay man), one Latino, and you're encouraged to think that's diversity.*"* —Holly Hughes

"Art is the most intense mode of individualism *the world has ever known."* —Oscar Wilde

"One writes out of one thing only—one's own experience. Everything depends on how relentlessly one forces from this experience the last drop, sweet or bitter, it can possibly give." —James Baldwin

"My gayness is an absolute, inextricable part of my persona and my art." —Frank Galati

"*[Raclyffe Hall's* The Well of Loneliness*] became my bible. I read it and reread it over and over again. And I vowed at that point that I was going to write a gay book that ended happily, a book about my people.*" —Nancy Garden

"*I don't know what goes on behind the scenes [in Hollywood], so I can't say for certain that I've never been the target of homophobia. But if I have, it hasn't affected me. I feel very fulfilled as an artist and as a man, and I'm excited about the creativity my work has brought about.*" —Dan Butler

"*I write the way I do because it's the way that gives me most pleasure, and which finds me my way into the poem.*"

—Marilyn Hacker

"I don't feel that [the gay scene] has much to offer me, but I try not to be too judgmental, because I do feel it has things to give to a younger generation. It's just sad that it can't be a scene that can encompass more shapes and sizes."

—Jimmy Somerville

"Gay culture is far from 'marginal,' being rather 'intersectional,' the conduit between unlike beings." —Judy Grahn

"I think it's a glamorous word, queer. I like the connotation of it. Gay is the most hideous word—its '30s connotation, when everyone had a gay time, I think was gross." —Rupert Everett

"I think to walk around and talk about gay-gay-gay would . . . trivialize who I am. Better to just be it and not talk about it."

—Steven Cojocaru

"To me, bad taste is what entertainment is all about."

—John Waters

"The gay label doesn't really bother me, as long as it's just not something that is restrictive. . . . I don't think that sexuality necessarily implies a lifestyle package that comes with it."

—*Neil Tennant of the Pet Shop Boys*

"Nothing could be more ridiculous than to say, as some critics have, that I am anti-homosexual simply because I do not embrace every twitty gay fad that comes along. I think that a lifetime of listening to disco music is a high price to pay for one's sexual preference." —*Quentin Crisp*

"Yes, it's very un-PC to categorize gay men as big drama queens, but unless you don't get out much it's a hard notion to outright dismiss." —*Patrick Price*

"When I grew up we had no positive images if we were gay. . . . All I knew about gays was that they always got beaten up in some Philip Marlowe movie." —*Harvey Fierstein*

"If it weren't for gays, honey, there wouldn't be a Hollywood!"

—*Elizabeth Taylor*

"*As with any group whose history bears deep scars, expressing ourselves culturally—particularly through the gay-influenced worlds of fashion and the arts—is not a simple issue of leisure. It's a passionate matter of survival.*" —Brendan Lemon

"*Gay culture is boring because gay culture is going away. And gay culture is going away because the oppression is going away. I think that's a pretty fair trade.*" —Dan Savage

"*If you removed all of the homosexuals and homosexual influence from what is generally regarded as American culture, you would be pretty much left with* Let's Make a Deal.*"*

—Fran Lebowitz

"*There's a part of me that really dreads assimilation. . . . I'm all for equality, but the idea of being assimilated to the point of losing my identity is just plain revolting to me.*" —Boy George

"*Achieving a well-accessorized Queer Identity is only a phase, not a destination, end product, or utopia, and it's time we stop treating it as such.*" —D. Travers Scott

"Our greatest hero in the entertainment world continues to be an apparent heterosexual—Madonna, who seems to wield even more power to impact change than all our closeted queer icons and do-nothing politicians combined." —*Michael Musto*

"What I reject is the idea that being a same-sexer means that you have to sign up for an identity, ideology, and a lifestyle in which everything is cut and dried and it's pre-digested. I think gay culture is part of the problem, not the solution."

—*Mark Simpson*

"My aim is to have an all-gay sitcom someday, with hetero-sexuals as token guest stars. Let them be the next-door neighbors for a change." —*Harvey Fierstein*

"If I had to choose one thing that exemplified gay culture over the past decade, it would have to be, for better or for worse, a sitcom." —*Andrew Holleran*

"I can . . . see what the gay community as an oppressed com-

munity has created, because every oppressed community always has the best culture going on—the best music, the best clothes, the best parties!" —Susie Bright

"What I try to do with my cartoons is document culture, but what is also happening is that I'm taking part in creating the culture." —Alison Bechdel

"I think people take dating too seriously. They approach it like a life or death situation, asking if this is 'the one' when they barely know the person's name." —Betty Berzon

"When sex is very good, sometimes, we can wonder what the difference is between sex and love. But the difference is clear."
—Alexander Chee

"Straight women are a lot more savvy about why they're attracted to us [queer women]. We know how to kiss." —Susie Bright

"I think that promiscuity has gotten a very bad name and some of the most intense and poetic and intimate experiences of my life were one-night stands." —Edmund White

"Some women can't say the word lesbian . . . even when their mouth is full of one." —Kate Clinton

"The sex act itself is neither male nor female: it is a human being reaching out for the ultimate in communication with another human being." —Del Martin and Phyllis Lyon

"I believed that the best way to get to know a woman was to go to bed with her . . . so pretty much everywhere I've lived I've had a real bad reputation. But it has gotten me a lot of interesting dates." —Dorothy Allison

"The most radical contribution the gay movement has made to society is the idea that pleasure justifies sexuality at least as much as reproduction." —Pat Califia

"Going into a gay bar expecting to meet another single guy and start a healthy relationship is like arranging a commitment ceremony on Rentboy.com." —Mike Albo

"I have no problem with my sexuality. I have a problem getting laid." —Bruce Vilanch

"If the religious right really wanted to stop gay sex, they should get behind gay people adopting, because nothing puts a stop to gay sex faster." —Dan Savage

"Sexual desire, I have argued in my work, is intensified rather than quelled by boundaries and taboos. Transgression is hot."
—Camille Paglia

"I'm a middle-class, educated, Jewish professor who cares about people and loves gay men. But that's not going to turn most men on. When I go to bars or sex spaces, leather and otherwise, I like to put on this image of a tough, blue-collar, rough, Italian-over-Jewish kind of badass. That turns men on."
—Eric Rofes

"I am not against sex. I am not telling each and everyone, You must live like this and this. I do not believe every gay person should be married, should be monogamous, should not be promiscuous." —Larry Kramer

"I . . . know the lack of game-playing that goes on between gay men. Men have that easy access to meaningless, casual sex, which gives them a totally different thrill [than straight men have]." —George Michael

"Sex is no miracle cure, but it can make one feel stronger, more alive, and connected to what those who are spiritually inclined might denominate as a higher power." —Ruthann Robson

"My body, heart, and soul have been a laboratory for research on the female orgasm." —Annie Sprinkle

"In its classic sense, On Our Backs is sort of the perfect expression of how subversive sex is, because having sex is about the only time you get to be on your back and calling the shots."
—Susie Bright, on the lesbian porn magazine she helped launch

"Pleasure is nature's test, her sign of approval." —Oscar Wilde

"My persona on camera is very dyke-friendly, and [the queer community] can tell I'm one of the best strap-on users in the business."
—Nina Hartley, on her queer visibility in her adult films

"The word bugger was never far from our lips. We discussed

copulation with the same excitement and openness that we discussed the good of nature."

—Virginia Woolf, on the Bloomsbury literary set

"The point of sexual relations between men is nothing that we could call love, but rather what we might call recognition."

—William S. Burroughs

"I believe that every member of Metropolitan Community Church must be sex-positive. Sex is Christianity's dirty little secret." —Rev. Troy D. Perry

"Retaining a Jewish identity [according to the Jewish Reconstructionist movement] is perceived as being far more important than whether or not someone is gay or lesbian."

—Rabbi Lisa Edwards

"I remain faithful to the church, but in its prohibition of homosexual clergy, I believe the church is not faithful to the work of God's spirit." —Karen Dammann

"The difference between political activists [in mainstream gay lobbying groups] and people of faith is that the political activists take on only what they believe they can win."

—Rev. Mel White

"Alienated for so long from other Jews, deeply divided about my own homosexuality, I have felt myself twice strange: Jewish in

the gay community, gay in the Jewish community . . . [but] coming out as a Jew ultimately made it possible for me to come out as a gay man and then work at uniting the two identities."

—Lev Raphael

"Both the church and politics are corrupt, but I believe in democracy and I believe in the message of God's love."

—Virginia Apuzzo

"Although my parents were Jewish, we certainly didn't adhere to any principles of the religion, and holidays were marked only by the appearance of particular foods on the table. . . . I have been attracted to the female-loving principles of Wicca, but I can no more see myself dancing naked in a circle during a full moon than I can picture myself spending every Friday night in a synagogue." —Karla Jay

"Although we can very easily argue technically that the Bible does not condemn us, I don't try." —Ann Northrop

"In Canada, where church attendance has plummeted in recent years (from sixty percent weekly attendance in 1957, to about thirty percent today), acceptance of gay men and lesbians has grown rapidly, whereas in the U.S., where church attendance and belief in God remains robust, tolerance lags."

—Sean Saraq

"One thing that really pisses me off is that the church—that is supposed to represent the teachings of Jesus Christ, who never said a word about homosexuals and whose teachings are about equality and loving each other, and doing unto others—and you have the institution of the church preventing homosexuals from becoming ministers to help and love people. It's just a perversion of the teachings to me." —Emily Saliers

"While many people consider the act of 'coming out' to be restricted to the provenance of sexuality, in the ultra-secular worldview that predominates gay subculture today, coming out as 'religious' is often met with the same prejudice, hostility, and misinformation and misunderstanding as declaring one's

homosexuality can provoke in the heterosexual mainstream culture." —Lawrence Schimel

"It's always seemed to me as a person brought up in a Christian belief, and who still counts himself as a Christian, as really ironic that some of the chief haters of gay people masquerade as followers of Jesus. It's astonishing to me because I believe I do understand the message of Jesus." —Michael Kirby

"I am proud to be in a church which works to be a safe place for all of God's children." —Bishop V. Gene Robinson

"Although much has changed in the past few years as I have accepted my gayness, much remains the same. I am still a rabbi, and I am still deeply committed to God, Torah, and Israel. My religious life had always been directed by the desire to be a servant of the Lord. None of that has changed."

—Rabbi Steve Greenberg

"I am astonished to be told by [Glasgow, Scotland, Catholic]

Cardinal [Thomas] Winning that my sexuality is not good for me. . . . As a gay man I am perfectly happy with my sexuality and my life. I can honestly say that the deepest longings of my heart are satisfied." —Sir Elton John

"When I first discovered the truth about my Jewish heritage [after having been raised Catholic], I found that Orthodox and Conservative Jews did not exactly embrace me as a lesbian. 'Let's just put that aside,' a Conservative rabbi said when I told him I was gay. . . . Judaism, he believed, would cure me of my homosexuality." —Helen Fremont

"Christian groups have insulted gays so often and for so many years with such negativity that my only hope is that we don't issue an insulting statement about gays at this conference. . . . It is a justice issue that is just as compelling as being opposed to apartheid in South Africa or to genocide in Rwanda."

—Episcopalian bishop Jack Spong, at a 1998 gathering of
Anglican bishops in Canterbury, England

"God does not despise anything that God has created."

—John J. McNeill

"One should no more deplore homosexuality than left-handed-ness." —1963 statement by English Quakers

"Dignity's [a gay Catholic group] mission is to help lesbian, gay, bisexual and transgender people to follow the ideal of Christians throughout the centuries: to be prayerful, respect-ful, honest, fair, forgiving, compassionate, and joyful—like the gay abbot, St. Aelred of Rievaulx, and like the martyr for conscience who dressed like a man, St. Joan of Arc."

—Daniel A. Helminiak

"My Zionism was . . . in direct opposition to my being queer, because my understanding was that if I wanted to be part of my people in Israel, then I had to be heterosexual, as well. Now I see many more options there." —Jenifer Levin

"I believe probably as much of the Church's official teaching as the Pope does . . . but we interpret it very differently."

—John Boswell

"The eight Biblical references (and not a single one by Jesus) to alleged homosexuality are very small indeed when compared to the several hundred references (and many by Jesus) to money and the necessity for justly distributing wealth. Yet few people go on a rampage about the issue of a just economic system, using the Bible as a base." —Suzanne Pharr

FAMILY:
BIOLOGICAL AND OTHERWISE

"I would rather feel exhilarated about the loves that constitute the fabric of my life than nostalgic for some tame ideal of what it means to be family." —Catherine Saalfield

"Gay friendships often create an alternative to family, a link more compelling than blood." —David Bergman

"You would think that those who are always talking about family values would want to create an environment of permanent relationships for people of the same sex. But they're not advocating family values. . . . They just are haters, period."
—Willie Brown

"You can't expect parents to accept everything instantly and unconditionally when it's taken you years to understand your own feelings. It's shocking sometimes to realize this, but our parents aren't superhuman." —Patrick Price

"My mother is an unrepentant old harridan. At her weakest with the chemo, she managed to remind me that if I lost weight, I might still be able to find a husband." —Alison Bechdel

"Having a gay child pits the instinct of parental love against entrenched social norms. To resolve the conflict, family members need to find answers to questions about human values and the meaning of personal integrity." —Bishop Melvin Wheatley

"[She went to make tea.] It was the classic English response. You know it's bad when they make tea."

—Andrew Sullivan, *on coming out to his mother*

"My parents are very supportive of me. . . . I was never in the closet, anyway, but I think that, within a family that's heterosexual, you're always going to be an outsider if you're gay."

—Jason Gould

"I think you're missing the silver lining here. When you're old and in diapers, a gay son will know how to keep you away from chiffon and backlighting."

—Megan Mullally as Karen from Will and Grace

"I was never quiet about having a gay son. I'd tell strangers. I

didn't care. I figured this was one way to educate people."

—Jeanne Manford

"I [came out to my family on] Thanksgiving. I said, 'Mom, would you please pass the gravy to a homosexual?' She passed it to my father. A terrible scene followed." —Bob Smith

"Any home where there is love constitutes a family and all families should have the same legal rights, including the right to marry and have or adopt children. Why shouldn't gay people be able to live as open and freely as everybody else?"

—Elizabeth Taylor

"Try not to take it personally—people don't know how to deal with what they don't understand. Just hold on to the belief that one day you'll be on your own and be able to make a life for yourself." —E. Lynn Harris, on how young GLBT people can deal with their homophobic parents

"Gay men's roles in parenting children profoundly affect not only their lives but the lives of the children they are rearing, as

well as the lives of gay men who continue to have a desire to parent but think that they cannot solely because they are gay, not to mention the larger heterosexual society." —Gary Mallon

"Their main concern was if I was going to be happy and that I was getting a divorce." —Chrissy Gephardt, daughter of U.S. Rep. Dick Gephardt, on coming out to her parents

"My parents always gave me the impression there is nothing I can't do." —Rob Weisbach

"I can introduce anyone I've slept with to anyone in my family, and I would have no embarrassment. They might not always be great dinner guests, however." —Alexis Arquette

"America has watched me parent my children on TV for six years. They know what kind of parent I am." —Rosie O'Donnell

"I meant it when I said I'd like to have a baby. I was deadly serious. I don't think it matters whether you're gay or not."

—Boy George

"[My parents] wish I was drawing Charlie Brown and making a zillion dollars a year, but they're supportive. As it happens, my mother is the Illinois Secretary of Arts and Culture and works with a bunch of gay men, so they kind of gleefully bring her the Ethan strip from the Chicago gay paper each week."

—Eric Orner

"I had to tell him that I couldn't not be out. The nicest thing about him is, he's so supportive and easy to educate, and he eventually saw things my way."

—Dr. Peter Shalit, on his dad, film critic Gene Shalit

"When asked, 'Shall I tell my mother I'm gay?' I reply, 'Never tell your mother anything.'" —Quentin Crisp

"Just by being out you're doing your part. It's like recycling. You're doing your part for the environment if you recycle; you're doing your part for the gay movement if you're out."

—Martina Navratilova

"The best thing you can do in your life is to stop lying, be honest, be true to yourself and what is important in your life. . . . If I've helped a few other young women to come out and be honest with their lives, then that is great." —Linda Villarosa

"If a bullet should enter my brain, let that bullet destroy every closet door." —Harvey Milk

"If one kid coming out can say to their parents, 'Hey, you know the woman who sang "At Seventeen," she's gay too,' then I have achieved something good." —Janis Ian

"The most important political step that any gay man or lesbian can take is to come out of the closet. It's been proven that it is easier to hate us and to fear us if you can't see us."

—Amanda Bearse

"I told her to write what was in her heart, that so far as any effect upon myself was concerned, I was sick to death of ambiguities, and only wished to be known for what I was and to dwell with her in the palace of truth." —Una Troubridge, upon Radclyffe Hall's consulting her before writing The Well of Loneliness and outing them both.

"What happened to me is exactly the opposite of what closeted people fear: They think they'll lose everything if they come out. This did not happen to me at all. In fact, everything came back tenfold." —Melissa Etheridge

"As far as coming out, I never really did that exactly; I just went along with the time. I never pulled an Ellen in announcing 'I'm gay!' At every opening night, I just quietly brought a boyfriend on my arm." —Jerry Herman

"The community takes you totally for granted [if you've always been out]. On the other hand, if you are straight first, and then you get to be famous and then you come out, the gay community can't do enough for you." —Suzanne Westenhoefer

"I have never hidden my homoeroticism in my life or in my work, never been ashamed of it, but I meant to keep it in a kind of proportion to life." —*Paul Cadmus*

"Deep down, my mom had long suspected I was gay. . . . Much of her anger and hurt came from her sense of betrayal that she was the last to be told." —*Chastity Bono*

"There's no torment in coming out. The torment is in being in."
—*Armistead Maupin*

"I would beg anyone, any celebrity, to please come out. It is the most important thing you'll ever do to save lives."
—*Ellen DeGeneres*

"I came out for political reasons and also because I wanted to live my life a certain way. . . . I was always telling my friends that it's possible to come out at the beginning of your career and still be successful." —*Wilson Cruz*

"I've always kept it fairly open without being brazen. And in the weird way this business works, when you're a character actor no one seems to care." —Denis O'Hare

"I came out really young. . . . I went straight from my mum's womb onto the gay parade." —Alexander McQueen

"Although [coming out is] going to make problems, those problems are not so dangerous as the problems of lying to yourself, to your friends, and missing many opportunities."

—Bayard Rustin

"When you come out, you change—utterly. You are for the first time yourself. And what has an actor got to use onstage but himself?" —Sir Ian McKellen

"I never officially came out in any kind of really public way. I just always lived very simply and openly, but the press has never made a big fuss about me or said anything to me." —Lily Tomlin

"I didn't come out until I was thirty-eight. I was able to be a lesbian because of the feminist and lesbian movement. Once I came out I felt like I had been given another opportunity in my life." —Nancy Bereano

"It is the closet that is our sin and our shame." —Barbara Grier

"The more of us [lesbians of color] that come out the stronger we are going to be, and the more other women are going to feel they are able to come out, because we are creating that kind of a situation where it is possible." —Pratibha Parmar

"I had no trouble after I learned that I was queer." —W. H. Auden

"My role as an AIDS celebrity just gives me a more elevated promontory from which to watch the world make the same mistakes in the handling of the AIDS epidemic that I had hoped my work would help to change." —Randy Shilts

"I was relieved [when I found out I was HIV positive] because once you've got it you can't catch it. I don't think I'm the kind of person who could get away with not being positive. I can't live like that—if I'd had to be vigilant up to this day, it would've killed me." —Aiden Shaw

"America is where I came out. I slept with half of it—and came out HIV-negative. I was a lucky, lucky person.... As long as I live, I will help fight [for] this cause." —Elton John

"There is absolutely no question whatsoever that protease inhibitors have helped people. But they've probably hurt more people than they've helped. That's why it's complicated.... the target population for the drug companies are the healthy people, and those people will almost certainly have their lives shortened by these drugs." —Dr. Joseph Sonnabend

"I'm an HIV-positive man who has done the unthinkable. I'm living my life. I'm having a ball." —Cole Tucker

"I think racism is a bottom-line AIDS issue. And I think homophobia is a bottom-line AIDS issue, and sexism and class issues and all of this. I think that we are not going to solve the AIDS epidemic unless we deal with these issues, and vice versa."
—Ann Northrop

"Listen, I can have a good time with the best of them, but I always find myself in the midst of those good times thinking about how many people are still dying of AIDS. I think we're in the midst of a false security." —Wilson Cruz

"About the criticism from activists that I don't do enough about AIDS? Well, enough is a bottomless pit. You can never do enough for a lot of people." —Greg Louganis

"In the beginning, when people got AIDS, we didn't know how they got it. But at this point they know, and for lesbians to con-

tinue to help people who are purposely infecting each other [via barebacking]—I think that's being codependent. It's enabling behavior that destroys people." —Robin Tyler

"Maybe if, instead of just seeing hot bodies having sex, people saw and read about the difficult drug regimens, the hunchbacks, the fat deposits, the soaring cholesterol levels . . . it might make them think more about staying safe."

—Michelangelo Signorile

"I have a beautiful address book a friend gave me in 1966. I literally cannot open it again. Ever. It sits on the shelf with over a hundred names crossed out. What is there to say? There are no words. I'll never understand why it happened to us."

—Jerry Herman

"I didn't want to hide this illness. I didn't want to live a lie. I've always wanted to be truthful."

—Rudy Galindo, on coming out as HIV-positive

"A lot of people who study HIV and STDs don't even think there is the potential of transmission between women because there's this incredible assumption that basically women don't have sex. It's the worst combination of sexism and homophobia."

—Dr. Jeanne Marrazzo

"I've lost over twenty friends [to AIDS]. I've seen a world vanish—a culture that has been oppressed in one generation, liberated in the next, and wiped out in the next." —Edmund White

"My life is a red ribbon. In fact, sometimes I feel like a big red ribbon with a little Paul Monette pinned to the lapel."

—Paul Monette

"It has been tremendously painful for me [to lose friends and patients to AIDS], because not only do I watch people I love die but I'm also in the fight as a doctor, and it's very hard to see something destroy so many people and not be able to stop it."

—Dr. Martin Palmer

"What disturbs me is how gay men all over this country can sit around with their friends dying, their lovers dying, their lives threatened, and not get off their asses and be activists again."
—Vito Russo

"Like some rabid animal, AIDS picked me up by the scruff of my neck, shook me senseless, and spat me out forever changed."
—Michael Callen

"Most of the activists, the AIDS activists who speak for us now, are so in the pockets of the bureaucracy of the drug companies that they have become almost fascist in ramming their treatment notions down the rest of us."
—Larry Kramer, in 2000

"The [AIDS] Quilt is the best thing I've ever done." —Cleve Jones

"The advent of AIDS made absolutely imperative an inflated level of sexual honesty." —Samuel Delany

QUEER POLITICS AND ACTIVISM

"We need political power to protect and defend ourselves as we work to eradicate homophobia. This answer may strike some as paranoid or simplistic; but the necessity of a movement that can defend queer people is urgent." —Urvashi Vaid

"The right wing is going to come down on women, and . . . on lesbians and gays, and we are going to be on the front line. But who is going to stand up for us on the campuses and in the community if we don't ourselves become multi-issued?"

—Merle Woo

"I'm gay, and as an elected city councilman I'm cost-effective. If I ever run for president, I can be my own first lady."

—Tom Ammiano

"I only started going to political rallies to meet women."

—k. d. lang

"All power is the willingness to accept responsibility."

—Larry Kramer

"No government has the right to tell its citizens when or whom to love. The only queer people are those who don't love anybody." —Rita Mae Brown

"The concerns over democracy and accountability are so serious that we urge people in the lesbian/gay/bisexual/transgender community to withhold their support and participation as well. Instead, we urge our brothers and sisters to continue our struggle in other ways—locally and nationally—that do not compromise our movement's principles." —New York City Council members Margarita Lopez, Christine Quinn, and Tom Duane, and New York Assembly member Deborah Glick, on why GLBT people should boycott the Millennium March on Washington

"The average American is less homophobic than he thinks he's supposed to be and more racist than he's willing to admit."
—Barney Frank

"Never doubt that we will create this world, because, my friends, we are fortunate to live in a democracy, and in a democracy, we decide what's possible." —Tammy Baldwin

"As a dyke in the Left before Stonewall and a high femme lesbian during the growth of lesbian feminism, my erotic yearnings were often in direct opposition to the very political movements I was committed to creating." —Amber Hollibaugh

"I've been an activist for a while and I know that the way to effect change is through moderation and through taking baby steps."
—Chastity Bono

"I wasn't a single-issue candidate. I didn't have a gay agenda. I mean, there's no 'gay' way to fill a pothole." —John Fiore

"Out of the chatrooms and into the streets! I do think that there are ways that we are connected through the Internet, but it's no substitute for actually getting out on the street and getting on your feet." —Kate Clinton

"If I do not fight bigotry wherever it is, bigotry is thereby strengthened. And to the degree that it is strengthened, it will, thereby, have the power to turn on me." —Bayard Rustin

"Groups like this do [gays and lesbians] a favor by keeping us in the public mind and giving us a visibility that we don't always do for ourselves."

—Betty Berzon, on the Traditional Values Coalition

"I'm not afraid to take a controversial position. If you don't piss off a few of your voters, you're not doing your job right."

—Tammy Baldwin

"It seems to me that [talking to straight men] is the one activist activity we all tend to shy away from." —Andrew Sullivan

"Once we each realize how much we can change ourselves, changing the world is easy."

—Calpernia Addams and Andrea James

"We can make sexual orientation a nonissue for the Republican Party, and we can help achieve equality for all gay and lesbian Americans." —Mary Cheney, daughter of Vice President Dick Cheney, in a public statement she issued on gay rights

"The American people finally seem willing to let us go to hell rather than jail." —Richard Goldstein

"I do believe that as an American citizen, a law-abiding, tax-paying citizen, that I should be allowed the same rights, the same pursuit of happiness that every other citizen enjoys."
—Melissa Etheridge

"If those who defend liberty are to be defined as conservative in today's political climate, then I'm proud to wear that label— as proud as I am of 'feminist,' 'gay,' and 'pro-choice.'"
—Tammy Bruce

"We don't yet have the political freedom to be able to be homo-sexuals only when we are making love with members of our own sex, but it is that freedom I know I'm working for." —Jane Rule

"Cultural work is political work when it's about taboo, or when it's about any area of shame. Shame is a great controller of people's dreams. And when you take on that shame, you're freeing people up for political struggle." —Joan Nestle

"I didn't think that in America I would have to choose between being honest and serving my country."

—Margarethe Cammermeyer

"Because we stand in the center of progress toward democracy, [gay people] have a terrifying responsibility to the whole society." —Bayard Rustin

"My lesbianism is the avenue through which I have learned the most about silence and oppression, and it continues to be the most tactile reminder to me that we are not free human beings." —Cherrie Moraga

QUEER HISTORY

"Almost all of my writing has been about empowerment and about trying to say to people of color, to women, to lesbians and gay men that you are really worth something, you are important, you have a history to be proud of. There is no reason to be ashamed." —Barbara Smith

"In the '50s and '60s, gay men seemed to despise one another. The idea of hanging out with another gay man was just not something you did." —Edmund White

"Lesbian history is strange. It is made up of many unknowable private facts and a few public inventions."

—Margaret Reynolds

"In 1967, I received a Ph.D. in English without the slightest notion that lesbian literature had a rich history and that many of the writers I admired had contributed to that history."

—Lillian Faderman

"Cross-dressing is a pattern in rebellions in far-flung countries.

And most importantly, this tradition appears to have ancient roots." —Leslie Feinberg

"Because the history of homosexuality has been denied or ignored, omitted in formal historical instruction and given no place in the family-centered oral traditions available to other disenfranchised groups, gay people's hunger for knowledge of their past is strong." —Martin Duberman

"Simple reason dictates that lesbians did exist widely in tribal cultures, for they exist now. . . . The concepts of tribal cultures and of modern, Western cultures are so dissimilar as to make ludicrous attempts to relate the long-ago women who dealt exclusively with women on sexual-emotional and spiritual bases to modern women who have in common an erotic attraction for other women." —Paula Gunn Allen

"Their relationships were a quasi-legitimate alternative to heterosexual marriage, and the participants did not describe them in the acknowledged sexual language—medical, reli-

gious, or pornographic—of the nineteenth century." —Esther
Newton, on members of the romantic friendships of the 1800s

*"To be a black woman poet in the '60s was to be invisible . . . triple
invisible as black, lesbian and feminist."* —Audre Lorde

*"In the '30s, the Nazi campaign against homosexuals was very
tightly directed toward gay men. Lesbians, if they were found
out, did face some severe consequences. But the only ones
who wore pink triangles and were sent to the camps were gay
men. So let's not take our politics and invent a past that
matches that."* —David Bianco

*"When I saw the success of the Third World student movement
[in the late 1960s], that radicalized me faster than dropping
Catholicism, faster than becoming a lesbian. . . . What changed
me was becoming conscious in a lightning flash that my education had been full of lies and censorship. I realized I had
never read anything by people of color."* —Merle Woo

"Between 1839 and 1842 Abraham Lincoln and Joshua Speed loved each other.... For years they shared a bed and their most private thoughts. They fell in love with each other and slept next to each other for four years." —Larry Kramer

"Gay culture is old, extremely old, and it is continuous. I have found that Gay culture has its traditionalist, its core group, that it is worldwide, and that it has tribal and spiritual roots."

—Judy Grahn

"The privatization of emotions and sexuality has been a primary form of social regulation. What happened in the public sphere was history, what happened in the private was, well, private."

—Michael Bronski

"An official, dominant, different-sex erotic ideal—a hetero-sexual ethic—is not ancient at all, but a modern invention. Our mystical belief in an eternal heterosexuality—our hetero-sexual hypothesis—is an idea distributed widely only in the last three-quarters of the twentieth century."

—Jonathan Ned Katz

"The massive war mobilization [during WWII] forced many American women and men to discover their homosexuality for the first time, to end their isolation in small towns and find other people like themselves, and to strengthen their identity as a minority in American society." —Allan Berube

"Whether or not [romantic friendships] had a genital component, the novels and diaries and correspondence of these periods consistently showed romantic friends opening their souls to each other and speaking a language that was in no way different from the language of heterosexual love."

—Lillian Faderman

"To live without history is to live like an infant, constantly amazed and challenged by a strange and unnamed world."

—Joan Nestle

"In the illumination of my own struggle around being black and gay and now HIV-positive, I wanted to connect to the communal struggle and to an historic struggle so that my story was not simply my story, but our story . . . for liberation, and redemption, and self-love." —*Marlon Riggs*

"*There have been few examples of repression of homosexuals in history as virulent as in Cuba.*"
—*Armando Valladares, in 1986*

GENDER IDENTITY:
BEYOND THE STEREOTYPES

"There are no pronouns in the English language as complex as I am, and I do not want to simplify myself in order to neatly fit one or the other." —Leslie Feinberg

"I jumped into drag like a kamikaze without stopping to think, who is this character, Mo B. Dick? Each time I did drag the character was developing and evolving."

—Mo B. Dick, aka Maureen Fischer

"Transsexual dressing is a gay contribution to the realization that we're not a hundred percent masculine or feminine, but a mixture of hormones." —Allen Ginsberg

"Everything would be better if we would institute a third pronoun." —Chloe Dzubilo

"Like I've always said, 'You're born naked and the rest is drag.' . . . I will not be ignored. I am here to stay." —RuPaul

"The more I get into the butch thing, the more I realize how

scared I am to wear a dress, and how when I wear one, I feel like a fag in drag." —*Lynn Breedlove*

"I hadn't even known the word 'transsexual,' nor that it was a word meant for me. In fact, I hadn't even known if trans-sexuals really existed, until at twenty-eight, I read Christine Jorgensen's book and finally admitted to being one."

—*Riki Ann Wilchins*

"It is not gender which causes problems; rather, it is the impo-sition of a gender on an individual by another. When the imposition is removed, polarity of masculine and feminine may remain, but as personal preference rather than imposed imperative." —*Nancy Nangeroni*

"I'll never get cast as a lesbian. I've been told that a million times. I don't look or act enough like a lesbian for them."

—*Suzanne Westenhoefer*

"I am still isolated as a transsexual man. There is still very little space for people like me in the community." —*Loren Cameron*

"While I talk about our rights to shape our own bodies and our own identities, I don't undress to do it." —Leslie Feinberg

"I'm not defined by what happened to me surgically. . . . I had all those things in me [already]." —Alexandra Billings

"One thing I think we must know—that our traditional gender roles will not be a part of the future, as long as the future is not a second Stone Age." —Joanna Russ

"All my life I've been taught that gender is something essential, something we're born with. Well, for the last decade or so, I've become increasingly convinced that gender is some sort of social construct." —Kate Bornstein

"I'm never sure if I have gender dysphoria or species dysphoria. I often try to explain that I'm really a starfish trapped in a human body and I'm very new to your planet."

—Pat[rick] Califia

"Our society at the moment is rolling the dice, instigated by gays, to reconsider what masculinity is and what makes a straight man or gay man, and if these definitions are real or if a middle ground can be found." —Brad Gooch

"You don't have to be a tranny to deviate from the rules of the gender game. You only have to act gay." —Richard Goldstein

"I knew I walked tough and sat with my legs apart and did not defer to men and boys, but I was a girl in the only way I knew how to be one." —Dylan (Daphne) Scholinski

"I consider myself 'transspecies': a hybrid blend of my own choosing. To me, the world is not just bi-gendered—there are a variety of genders." —Christopher Lee

"Discrimination against gay, lesbian, bisexual and transgendered people is all of a piece because it is rooted in people's assumptions about what it is to be male or female. . . . The amount of discrimination we face is often linked to how we look." —Kerry Lobel

"Why is it that when we meet someone the first thing we assess in order to relate to them is whether they are male or female? We cling to gender almost desperately, panicking when it is ambiguous or complicated, simply because we are somehow implicated in the confusion." —Guinevere Turner

"Never keep up with the Joneses; drag them down to your level. It's cheaper." —Quentin Crisp

"If homosexuality is a disease, let's all call in queer to work: 'Hello. Can't work today, still queer.'" —Robin Tyler

"What do you mean, you 'don't believe in homosexuality'? It's not like the Easter Bunny, your belief isn't necessary."
—Lea Delaria

"My lesbianism is an act of Christian charity. All those women out there praying for a man, and I'm giving them my share."
—Rita Mae Brown

"There is nothing wrong with going to bed with someone of your own sex. People should be very free with sex; they should draw the line at goats." —Elton John

"The next time someone asks you, 'Hey, howdja get to be a homosexual anyway?' tell them, 'Homosexuals are chosen first on

talent, then interview, then the swimsuit and evening gown competition pretty much gets rid of the rest of them.'

—Karen Williams

"I can't help looking gay. I put on a dress and people say, 'Who's the dyke in the dress?'" —Karen Ripley

"We've all heard the joke 'What do gay men do on the second date?' Punch line: 'What second date?'" —Patrick Price

"If male homosexuals are called 'gay,' then female homosexuals should be called 'ecstatic.'" —Shelly Roberts

"I don't think of them as lesbian supervisors, I think of them as county supervisors who happen to be lesbians. A lesbian supervisor would have a very different job: 'Hey you, cut those nails before you hurt somebody!'" —Marga Gomez

"I'm as pure as the driven slush." — Tallulah Bankhead

"Homophobia: The irrational fear that three fags will break into your house and redecorate it against your will."

—Tom Ammiano

"The Bible contains six admonishments to homosexuals and 362 to heterosexuals. This doesn't mean God doesn't love heterosexuals. It's just that they need more supervision."

—Lynn Lavner

"The first time I heard two lesbians talking about who's a top, who's a bottom, I said, 'What are they talking about—pajamas?'" —Karen Williams

"Since I was sixteen—the year I realized there were other teenage boys who had impure thoughts about Starsky and Hutch—*my rule of thumb with my father has been: He doesn't ask me about my love life, I shouldn't tell him anything he doesn't want to know, and, as a good son, I mustn't pursue anyone, even if he's tall, has a good job, and my mother (a woman who once called Bill Clinton and Al Gore 'a handsome couple') thinks he's cute."* —Frank Decaro

"Why can't they have gay people in the army? Personally, I think they are just afraid of a thousand guys with M16s going, 'Who'd you call a faggot?'" —Jon Stewart

"Memo to the operatives: Old gay agenda—world domination by 2001—has been scrapped. Look for a new gay agenda in your mailbox sometime in June." —Bruce Vilanch

"For everyone out there who thinks the theater is full of nothing but Jews and gays, all I have to say is, 'Oy gevalt, my lover and I just won a Grammy!'"

—Marc Shaiman, in his 2003 Grammy acceptance speech

"I like dogs [better than people]. . . . The difference between dogs and men is that you know where dogs sleep at night."

—Greg Louganis

"Can you imagine lesbian group sex? It would take three girls, two to do it and one to write a folksong about it." —Lea DeLaria

"I'd like to blame my atrocious appearance [in high school] on my trying to pass myself off as straight, but during the '70s even the gay people looked awful. We were the Bicentennial Class of 1976, and America seemed to be celebrating 200 years of bad hair." —Bob Smith

"I decided to do gay and lesbian comedy because I don't ever want to be rich and famous, and it's working." —Karen Ripley

"I didn't do drugs, I did Warner Bros. movies."
—Charles Busch, on his adolescence

"As a comic, I travel around a lot and I see a lot of road signs. And very often I see a sign that says ADOPT A HIGHWAY. When I see this sign, I always wonder, 'What if you're a lesbian? Is it legal to adopt a highway? Isn't there a danger that somehow you'd influence the highway and it would become a lesbian highway?'" —Sara Cytron

"If God had intended us to be athletes, he would have given us jockstraps." —Sir Ian McKellen

"Sports are great because they build butch self-esteem, and also give femmes a place to go and watch butches play!"
                                                        —JoAnn Loulan

"I don't have a problem with crashing and dying. I think being an athlete is in the mind. It's not in the body." —Missy Giove

"I don't understand boxing. . . . The goal is to draw blood and knock someone out. I just don't get it." —Greg Louganis

"The formula for success is simple: practice and concentration, then more practice and more concentration."
                                                        —Babe Didrikson

"I had finally gotten to the point where it was more important to be myself than a baseball player." —Glenn Burke

"Sport, with its physical empowerment and lesbian potential, is

an inherently feminist act." —Mariah Burton Nelson

"Softball is the single greatest organizing force in lesbian society." —Alix Dobkin

"The Gay Games define us as a coherent, diverse population asserting our right to celebrate ourselves—not ask for someone else's approval." —Ann Northrop

"Surely the most unexpected and most successful of the gay alternatives to straight sporting events is the most macho of all American activities of any sort, the rodeo."

—Perry Deane Young

"I cry at basketball games. When those guys touch each other—these presumably heterosexual men hugging each other and shit—I love it." —Reno

"I have to say that I am disappointed in my fellow gay players."
—Muffin Spencer-Devlin, on coming out among closeted golfers

"Football is all very well as a game for rough girls, but it is hardly suitable for delicate boys." —Oscar Wilde

"Lesbians sometimes don't realize that in women's basketball the pressure to conform to the heterosexual image hurts all women—gay or straight." —Kirsten Cummings

"If lesbians aren't part of the gestalt of the WNBA, I don't know who is." —Cathy Renna

"Sports has never been an institution willing to get too far ahead of the curve. Its approach is that within the framework of their organization, they're not interested in being controversial or daring." —Pat Griffin

"There remain gay umpires at every level of the sport who live with the contradictions [of being gay in the sports world] every day. . . . Professional sports is fueled by masculinity. The old stereotypes will linger until new images of gay men prove them wrong." —Tyler Hoffman

"Sports kept me in the closet because the norm is that you can't be gay when you play football. You can't be gay and be the star player." —Esera Tualo

"I called myself a rock climber, lived by climbing language and dress years before I knew I was a lesbian. It was the feel of cold hard rock biting into the tips of my fingers that made me rush into the day wanting more." —Susan Fox Rogers

"I think we just need to get the dialogue out there and not limit it only to the playing field but also open up the front office, the stadium workers, the scouts, the umpires—and then soon, the baseball players." —Billy Bean

"Rudy Galindo is the only out gay man in our sport. There are a lot more football players out than figure skaters. I've always known this but now I'm to the point [of] who really cares, anyway?" —Brian Boitano

"There's a conspiracy of quietness that comes from the NFL.

Don't tell me they don't know that gay men are active in the NFL." —David Kopay

"By submerging myself in boxing, I learned to be more comfortable with being myself—part of which meant being gay—and with being a man in general." —Mark Leduc

"Girls who put out are tramps. Girls who don't are ladies. This is, however, a rather archaic use of the word. Should one of you boys happen upon a girl who doesn't put out, do not jump to the conclusion that you have found a lady. What you have probably found is a lesbian." —Fran Lebowitz

"For a long time I thought I wanted to be a nun. Then I realized that what I really wanted to be was a lesbian." —Mabel Maney

"A butch/femme couple is queer. They do not meet social expectations even if they live exemplary role-differentiated lives—lesbians from Leave It to Beaver. *In fact, the more gender differentiation in their relationship, the queerer they are."*
—Carol Queen

"I think the reason butch-femme stuff got hidden within lesbian feminism is because people are profoundly afraid of questions of power in bed." —Amber Hollibaugh

"Every woman I have ever loved has left her print upon me,

where I loved some invaluable piece of myself apart from me—so different that I had to stretch and grow in order to recognize her." —Audre Lorde

"Lesbian existence comprises both the breaking of a taboo and the rejection of a compulsory way of life. It is also a direct or indirect attack on male right of access to women."

—Adrienne Rich

"If a straight woman falls in love with me, she must really love me. If a gay woman loves me, she's just a lesbian looking for a girlfriend." —Sarah Schulman

"Butch women are exciting women. Their power, the sexual excitement—there's a lot of romance and mystery. Butches are exciting. Beebo is one of them."

—Ann Bannon, on her 1950s pulp butch character Beebo Brinker

"My only books were women's looks."

—Natalie Barney, on her education

"When I came out, I didn't even get that you were a lesbian for sexual reasons. It was almost like another political challenge."
—Susie Bright

"I count the support and encouragement of women as my primary motivation for writing." —Cheryl Clarke

"My lesbianism is not linked to sexual preference. For me, it is part of my world view, part of my passion for women and central in my objection to male domination." —Holly Near

"One of the qualities she admired in certain lesbian relationships was the ability of women not only to enjoy the ecstasy of orgasm but to cultivate a more diffused and warm sensuality."
—Jane Rule, on the writer Colette

"[In college] I was a feminist trying to come out, and there were, like, three lesbians in Kalamazoo, and they were all involved with each other! I often say I came to New York to be a feminist artist, but I really came hoping to get laid!" —Holly Hughes

"It's fine with me if people think I'm a lesbian."

—Janeane Garofalo

"I am a lesbian, not a woman." —Monique Wittig

"I'm the person most likely to sleep with my female fans. I genuinely love other women. And I think they know that."

—Angelina Jolie

"Ours is a society that disregards girls, that renders them invisible. I want to write against this invisibility and explore social issues important to their existence."

—Jacqueline Woodson

"As a writer, I am very concerned with language. When I say I'm a dyke, I mean dyke, not lesbian, not female homosexual, not gay woman." —Laura Antoniou

"I have lesbian impulses, so I understand how a man looks at a woman." —Camille Paglia

"By my *definition I am a 'lesbian' in that I have loved women and will continue to love them sexually, politically, and spiritually—it's very much a political statement for me, it's not the rigid limitations of some kind of biological choice, like: 'I only sleep with women.'"* —Sapphire

"Don't they know I'm a gay man trapped in a woman's body?"

—Madonna, on her critics

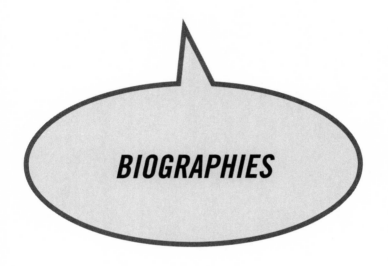

BIOGRAPHIES

Addams, Calpernia: Performer, writer, and artist, and cofounder and co-owner of production company Deep Stealth. Addams was portrayed in the 2003 Showtime film *Soldier's Girl*, which told the story of her relationship with Pfc. Barry Winchell; Winchell was murdered by two of his fellow soldiers when they discovered Addams was transgender.

Addams, Jane (1860–1935): Activist, feminist, writer, and founder of Hull House, one of the first settlement houses in the U.S. Addams, who maintained long-term relationships with at least two women during her lifetime, was a suffragette and social reformer, and published numerous books on both Hull House and the effects of industrialization.

Albo, Mike: Writer, comedian, and performer. Albo is the author of the 2000 novel *Hornito: My Lie Life*, contributes to numerous magazines and newspapers, and has done several solo shows.

Allen, Paula Gunn (1939–): Educator and author of numerous books of poetry, novels, and essays, many of which focus on Native American culture. Allen was among the first scholars to explore two-spirit identity and lives in her works, which include *Hwame, Koshkalak, and the Rest: Lesbians in American Indian Cultures* (1981) and *The Sacred Hoop: Recovering the Feminine in American Indian Traditions* (1986).

Allison, Dorothy (1949–): Best-selling, critically lauded author of numerous novels, including 1992's *Bastard Out of Carolina* and 1998's *Cavedweller*. Allison has also published poetry collections, essay collections, and short stories, many of which explore themes of queer identity, sex, and socioeconomic status.

Almodovar, Pedro (1949–): Spanish filmmaker whose queer-tinged films include *All About My Mother* (1999), *Matador* (1986), and *Kika* (1981). The commercially successful, prolific Almodovar, who describes his sexuality as fluid, has also written fiction and acted in theater.

Ammiano, Tom: Openly gay president of the San Francisco Board of Supervisors and stand-up comic. Formerly a teacher, Ammiano ran for mayor in San Francisco in 2003.

Antoniou, Laura: Writer, editor, and activist. Antoniou openly identifies as a sadomasochist and has published several books and anthologies on lesbian S/M issues, including 1995's *No Other Tribute* and 1996's *Some Women*.

Apuzzo, Virginia (1941–): Accomplished civil rights advocate, government official, and former president of the National Gay Task Force (NGTF) (1982–1986). An openly gay politician, she was a delegate to the 1980 and 1985 Democratic National Conventions.

Arquette, Alexis (1969–): Actor who has starred in several independent films, including *Wigstock* (1995) and *Love Reinvented* (2000). Arquette is the openly gay brother of actors Patricia, Rosanna, and David Arquette.

Auden, W. H. (Wystan Hugh) (1907–1973): Prominent British poet. Much of Auden's poetry celebrated romantic love and he was a leading voice of his generation. Although he rejected the label of "gay poet," his controversial 1948 poems "A Day for a Lay" and "Fire Island" were explicitly homoerotic, and he partnered with the American Chester Kallman for most of his adult life.

Baldwin, James (1924–1987): Hugely influential African-American gay writer and intellectual. Author of the 1956 gay classic *Giovanni's Room*, one of the first novels to openly address homosexuality, Baldwin wrote twenty-one other published books over the span of his distinguished career, and was a popular public speaker on civil rights.

Baldwin, Tammy (1962–): Democratic U.S. Congress member and lawyer. Baldwin was elected to the Wisconsin state assembly in 1993 and moved up to U.S. Representative in 1999; she was not only the youngest state representative ever, but also the first openly gay person to serve.

Bankhead, Tallulah (1903–1968): Actor of the 1930s and 1940s who appeared in plays including *The Little Foxes* (1939) and films including *Lifeboat* (1944) and *A Royal Scandal* (1945). Though some of her work met with success, she seems to be best remembered for her scandalous behavior and sexual liaisons with other women rather than her acting.

Bannon, Ann (Ann Thayer) (1932–): Educator and author of the Beebo Brinker series of lesbian pulp novels, published in the 1950s and 1960s. Bannon's books continue to stand out for their honest and moving portrayal of New York City lesbian life of earlier decades.

Barney, Natalie Clifford (1877–1972): American-born writer who lived her adult life in Paris. Barney ran an artists' salon and became infamous for her dramatic affairs with other women, including painter Romaine Brooks.

Beam, Joseph (1954–1988): Writer and editor who worked toward the empowerment of African-American gay men. Beam was a board member of the National Coalition of Black Lesbians and Gays, and edited a 1986 anthology of black gay literature called *In the Life*.

Bean, Billy (1964–): Former Major League baseball player for the Tigers, Dodgers, and Padres who came out in 1999. His autobiography, *Going the Other Way*, was published in 2003.

Bearse, Amanda (1958–): Actor and director who came out as a lesbian in 1993, while a cast member of the television show *Married . . . with Children*.

Bechdel, Alison (1960–): Cartoonist and creator of well-known lesbian comic strip "Dykes to Watch Out For," which has run in queer newspapers for over twenty years and has been collected into Lambda Literary Award ("Lammy")-winning books.

Bereano, Nancy (1941–): Founder and publisher of Firebrand Press (1984–2000), which published many groundbreaking lesbian and feminist books, including the works of Dorothy Allison, Alison Bechdel, Audre Lorde, and Minnie Bruce Pratt. Bereano won a Publisher's Service Award at the 1996 Lammys.

Bergman, David: Author and poet whose books include 2003's *Violet Hour: The Violet Quill and the Making of Gay Culture* and the George Ellison Poetry Prize-winning volume *Cracking the Code* (1986). Bergman has also edited numerous anthologies, and teaches English at Towson State University.

Bernhard, Sandra (1955–): Comedian, writer, singer, and actor who has appeared in film and on television as well as in her own solo shows, and is highly visible in queer culture. She received a Grammy nomination for the recording of her 1988 show *Without You I'm Nothing* and has published several autobiographical books.

Berube, Allan: Historian, activist, and writer who is noted for his contributions to gay and lesbian studies. He authored the award-winning 1990 book *Coming Out Under Fire: The History of Gay Men and Women in World War II*, which was the basis for a 1993 documentary, and earned a MacArthur Fellowship in 1996.

Berzon, Betty (1928–): Psychotherapist and writer of GLBT-themed nonfiction books on positive gay identity and relationships, including *Permanent Partners: Building Gay and Lesbian Relationships That Last* (1998). Berzon helped to found the very first gay community center in Los Angeles.

Bianco, David: The founder of Q Syndicate, which provides queer content to the GLBT press, Bianco is also the author of several books, including 1999's *Gay Essentials: Facts for Your Queer Brain* and *Past Out*, a widely published newspaper column.

Billings, Alexandra (1962–): Actress, writer, and cabaret singer who has appeared in numerous theatrical productions, including Larry Kramer's *Just Say No* (1999). She is the winner of several After Dark Awards and made history as the first transgender woman to play a transgender female character on television.

Boitano, Brian (1963–): Olympic gold-medal figure skater who won four consecutive U.S. titles (1985–1988) before turning pro. Boitano was the first—and so far only—male skater to be featured by himself on the cover of *Sports Illustrated.*

Bono, Chastity (1969–): Activist and out lesbian daughter of Cher and Sonny Bono. Bono is the author of two memoirs, 1998's *Family Outing* and 2002's *The End of Innocence.*

Bornstein, Kate (1948–): Openly transgender writer and performance artist who has written extensively about gender identity in hir (Bornstein's preferred pronoun) work, including hir books *Gender Outlaw: On Men, Women, and the Rest of Us* (1995) and *My Gender Workbook* (1998).

Boswell, John (1947–1994): Controversial historian and writer whose groundbreaking 1980 book *Christianity, Social Tolerance, and Homosexuality* helped establish him as a major critic of constructionist theory. He was also a founder of Yale's Lesbian and Gay Studies Center in 1987.

Brant, Beth (1941–): Lesbian Native American writer of stories and poems, mainly about experiences of gay and lesbian Natives. Brant is also an activist and archivist, and editor of the highly successful 1983 anthology *A Gathering of Spirit: A Collection by North American Indian Women.*

Breedlove, Lynn (1959–): Performer, writer, and educator. Breedlove is the vocalist for San Francisco-based dyke-punk band Tribe 8, wrote the acclaimed 2002 novel *Godspeed*, and has taught at the Harvey Milk Institute.

Bright, Susie (1956–): Editor and writer also known as "Susie Sexpert." Bright is the author of numerous books on sex and sexual politics, including 1990's *Susie Sexpert's Lesbian Sex World* and 1999's *Full Exposure: Opening Up to Sexual Creativity and Erotic Expression*, and a founder of the successful lesbian sex magazine *On Our Backs*.

Broadwell, Charles: *New York Times* editor and publisher who was in control of the paper when it decided to begin running same-sex union announcements in its wedding pages.

Bronski, Michael (1945–): Cultural critic and author of groundbreaking books such as 1985's *Culture Clash: The Making of a Gay Sensibility* and 1999's *The Pleasure Principle*. Bronski became active with the gay liberation movement of the 1960s and has been widely published in various periodicals.

Brown, Rita Mae (1944–): Author of the classic lesbian novel *Rubyfruit Jungle* (1983) as well as numerous other books, including mysteries, poetry collections, essays, articles, and screenplays. Brown was involved in the civil rights movement in the 1960s and remains active in the struggle for gay and lesbian rights.

Brown, Willie (1934–): Mayor of San Francisco from 1996 to 2003, Brown has also been the longest-serving Speaker of the California State Assembly (serving from 1980 to 1995). He was the city's first African-American mayor and the only African-American Speaker in California history.

Bruce, Tammy: Conservative, out lesbian author of 2001's *The New Thought Police: Inside the Left's Assault on Free Speech and Free Minds* and a Fox News Channel contributor. Bruce was the youngest NOW chapter president ever elected and once hosted a radio talk show in Los Angeles.

Burke, Glenn (1952–1995): Outfielder for the Los Angeles Dodgers from 1976 to 1978 and the Oakland A's from 1978 to 1980. Burke, the originator of the "high-five," was the first pro baseball player to come out.

Burroughs, William S. (1914–1997): Subversive gay writer of the Beat Generation who is known not only for his literary works but for his experimentation with sex and drugs. His hallucinatory 1959 novel *The Naked Lunch* and 1953's hard-boiled *Junkie* have become classics.

Busch, Charles (1954–): Playwright and actor who wrote and starred in the off-Broadway production *The Lady in Question* (1989), the long-running hit *Vampire Lesbians of Sodom* (1986, also off-Broadway), and the Tony-nominated Broadway hit *The Tale of the Allergist's Wife* (2001), for which he won the Outer Circle Critics John Gassner Award. He has written numerous other works, long performed in gay theater, and been the recipient of such honors as the Drama Desk Award in 2003.

Butler, Dan (1954–): Actor who has appeared in several films as well as on the sitcom *Frasier* as Bob "Bulldog" Briscoe. Butler, who is openly gay, also wrote and performed in an off-Broadway autobiographical show entitled *The Only Thing Worse You Could Have Told Me* (1994).

Byron, George Gordon, Lord (1788–1824): Legendary British poet whose work is considered great not only now, but was also immensely popular during his time. Although he was not outed as bisexual until well after his death, Byron conducted a number of affairs with—and wrote romantic poems about—other young men.

Cadmus, Paul (1904–): American artist, known as a "magical realist," whose provocative 1933 painting of sailors entitled *The Fleet's In!* drew controversy. Many of his later paintings, including *The Bath* (1951) and *What I Believe* (1947–1948), also feature homoerotic imagery and pushed the limits of what was then deemed acceptable in art.

Califia, Pat(rick) (1954–): Openly transgender writer, activist, and sex radical whose work—including nonfiction books like 1980's *Sapphistry: The Book of Lesbian Sexuality*, 1994's *Public Sex*, and novels such as 1990's *Doc and Fluff*—has focused largely on queer sex and the politics of S/M.

Callen, Michael (1955–1993): Singer-songwriter, AIDS activist, and writer. Callen was a member of The Flirtations, a gay male a cappella singing group; helped found numerous AIDS organizations; and wrote the 1990 book *Surviving AIDS*, which received an honorable mention from the American Medical Writers Association.

Cameron, Loren (1959–): Openly transgender photographer and body-builder who documented his transition from female to male. His ground-breaking 1996 book of self-portraits, *Body Alchemy*, received critical praise and two Lammys.

Cammermeyer, Margarethe (1943–): A former army colonel, Cammermeyer served as a military nurse for twenty-six years, headed the Washington State National Guard's nursing corps for several years, and received a Bronze Star before being discharged from the service because of her lesbianism. Her 1994 memoir *Serving in Silence* was later made into a TV movie.

Capote, Truman (Truman Streckfus Persons) (1924–1984): Acclaimed writer whose first novel, 1948's *Other Voices, Other Rooms,* was a critical smash and whose other books including 1958's *Breakfast at Tiffany's* and the 1966 "nonfiction novel" *In Cold Blood* were hugely successful. Capote was out as a gay man throughout his career.

Chee, Alexander (1967–): Writing teacher and out author of the critically praised, Lammy-winning 2001 novel *Edinburgh*.

Cheney, Mary: Out lesbian daughter of Vice President Dick Cheney. Formerly the Coors Brewing Company's liaison to the gay community, Cheney left Coors to pursue an MBA at the University of Colorado.

Clarke, Cheryl (1947–): Writer whose poetry and essays have explored the duality of her lesbian and African-American identities, and have appeared in numerous journals and anthologies. She is the Director of the Office of Diverse Community Affairs and Lesbian-Gay Concerns at Rutgers University and the author of *Living as a Lesbian* (1986) and *Experimental Love* (1993), among other books.

Clinton, Kate (1951–): A comedian and writer who has been performing publicly since 1981. Clinton was one of the first openly queer comics on television. She has recorded six comedy albums, writes monthly columns for *The Advocate* and *The Progressive*, and has taught and lectured widely on humor writing and the uses of humor in effecting cultural change.

Cocteau, Jean (1889–1963): French artist and writer whose interdisciplinary work in theater, film, ballet, poetry, and fashion was extensive. Cocteau was not publicly out, though widely known to be gay; his 1928 nonfiction book *Le Livre Blanc* contained explicit details of his sexual relationships with men.

Cojocaru, Steven (1969–): Fashion writer known for his campy style and wit. The author of *The Red Carpet Diaries* (2003), he is currently a correspondent for *Entertainment Tonight*, weekly contributor to the *Today* show, and columnist and West Coast Style Editor for *People* magazine.

Coward, Sir Noel (1899–1973): British playwright, actor, screenwriter, producer, singer, and songwriter whose homosexuality was an "open secret" in London during his day. Many of his works, which include *The Vortex* (1924), *Private Lives* (1930), and *Design for Living* (1933), have a campy sensibility and subtly explored themes of being closeted.

Crisp, Quentin (Denis Crisp) (1908–1999): British writer, actor, and performance artist whose scathing wit made him an unforgettable queer icon. His 1968 memoir *The Naked Civil Servant* brought him infamy in England as a "self-evident homosexual." He later emigrated to the U.S. and became a celebrity there as well.

Cruz, Wilson (1974–): Out gay actor and singer best known for his portrayal of the "sexually confused" teen Rickie Velazquez on the '90s television show *My So-Called Life*. He has since appeared in shows and in films, including 1997's *All Over Me*.

Cummings, Kirsten: Openly lesbian basketball player who played professionally abroad before joining the American Basketball League.

Cytron, Sara: Stand-up comic who performed lesbian feminist material written by her partner, Harriet Malinowitz, for over a decade. She also had experience as a director and made television appearances before leaving the comedy world to study law.

Dammann, Karen (1957–): Methodist minister who had charges brought against her—and later dropped—by the church after coming out as a lesbian.

Davies, Russell (1963–): Accomplished TV writer and creator of the original British *Queer as Folk* television series.

de Beauvoir, Simone (1908–1986): French writer and philosopher and author of the classic feminist work *The Second Sex* (1949). Though her relationship with Jean-Paul Sartre was well-known, Beauvoir documented several same-sex relationships in her journals.

Decaro, Frank (1962–): Openly gay writer and comedian who hosts an "Out at the Movies" segment on Comedy Central's *The Daily Show*, writes for the *New York Times* and numerous other publications, and is a consulting editor at *TV Guide*. His memoir, *A Boy Named Phyllis*, was published in 1996.

DeGeneres, Ellen (1958–): Comedian and actor who famously came out as a lesbian in 1997 on her sitcom *Ellen*. Though the show was cancelled shortly afterward, DeGeneres found success in several films including 2003's *Finding Nemo*, as well as with her recent television talk show.

Delany, Samuel (1942–): Writer and theorist who is also an outspoken advocate for sexual openness. In addition to his gay-themed memoirs and journal articles, Delany is the author of such novels as 1967's *The Einstein Intersection* and 1984's *Stars in My Pocket like Grains of Sand*, and has won numerous Nebula Awards for science fiction.

Delaria, Lea (1958–): Openly gay comedian, singer, and actor who met with success in stand-up and went on to make film and television appearances. She had a major role in the 1998 film *Edge of Seventeen* and appeared on Broadway in both the musical *On the Town* and *The Rocky Horror Picture Show*, to rave reviews.

Denneny, Michael (1943–): Editor, writer, and queer publishing pioneer who published the works of Randy Shilts and Larry Kramer, among others. Founder of St. Martin's Press' gay-themed paperback imprint Stonewall Inn Editions and cofounder of gay literary magazine *Christopher Street*, Denneny is also the author of *Lovers* (1979).

Didrikson, Babe (Mildred Ella Didrikson) (1911–1956): American athlete who excelled in nearly every sport; won two gold medals and a rare gold-silver medal in the 1932 Olympics; was a six-time winner of the Associated Press Woman Athlete of the Year award; and helped found the Ladies Professional Golf Association. Though she married a man, it was widely speculated that she maintained intimate relationships with women.

DiMassa, Dianne (1961–): Creator of the comic book zine *Hothead Paisan: Homicidal Lesbian Terrorist* and illustrator of numerous books. DiMassa founded Giant Ass Publishing in 1991 in order to publish quarterly issues of *Hothead*, which consistently sold out in bookstores; two book-length collections of the comics were later published.

Ditto, Beth: Out singer for Olympia-based queercore band The Gossip. Ditto's lyrics reflect her outspokenness about identifying as "fat and queer and femme."

Dobbs, Bill: Longtime gay-rights and AIDS activist, lawyer, and media critic. Dobbs worked with ACT UP and is a founder of and spokesman for Queer Watch, an organization of gay grassroots activists who oppose the death penalty.

Dobkin, Alix (1940–): Lesbian feminist women's music pioneer who founded the record label Women's Wax Works. Dobkin was a member of the all-female band Lavender Jane, whose 1973 album *Lavender Jane Loves Women* broke ground as the first record put together start to finish exclusively by lesbians. She has also released numerous solo albums.

Duane, Tom (1955–): Democratic New York State Senator in Manhattan who became the Senate's first openly gay and HIV-positive member in 1998. Before his election, he was a member of the New York City Council for seven years; he also ran for Congress in 1994 but was unsuccessful.

Duberman, Martin (1930–): Historian, writer, and educator. Duberman has published numerous books, including his memoirs and *Stonewall*, his 1993 account of the Stonewall uprisings. He is the recipient of multiple awards and was a founding member of the Lambda Legal Defense and Education Fund and the National Gay Task Force (later NGLTF).

Dzubilo, Chloe (1961–): Out transgender New York City-based singer, writer, and AIDS activist. Dzubilo was the lead singer for the band the Transisters in the '90s and is the founder of Equi-Aid, a horseback riding program for at-risk inner-city youth.

Edwards, Rabbi Lisa: Out lesbian who has been a rabbi with Beit Chayim Chadasheim, a GLBT-inclusive synagogue in Los Angeles, since 1994.

Etheridge, Melissa (1961–): Rock musician. She is the recipient of two Gramy Awards, and her 1993 platinum album *Yes I Am* was released the year she came out as a lesbian.

Everett, Rupert (1959–): British film actor who has been out since 1989 and appeared—as a gay character—in American movies such as 1997's *My Best Friend's Wedding* and 2000's *The Next Best Thing*.

Faderman, Lillian (1940–): Writer, historian, and educator whose contributions to the lesbian and gay studies canon include 1981's *Surpassing the Love of Men*, 1991's *Odd Girls and Twilight Lovers*, and 1999's *To Believe in Women*. A respected scholar, Faderman teaches English and Lesbian Studies at California State University.

Fallon, Ed: Democratic State Representative in Iowa who is considering running for governor in 2006.

Feinberg, Leslie (1949–): Political organizer, historian, and writer who has long been an important voice in transgender activism and culture. Feinberg's 1993 novel *Stone Butch Blues* is a favorite among GLBT readers, and won both a Lammy and an American Library Association Award for Gay and Lesbian Literature.

Feinstein, Michael (1956–): Pianist and singer who has recorded over twenty albums, two of which received Grammy nominations. The openly gay Feinstein has also performed on television and in film, and in 1999 he opened his own club in Manhattan.

Fiore, John: Former urban planner and member of the City Council of Wilton Manors, Florida, who became the municipality's first openly gay mayor in 2000.

Fierstein, Harvey (1954–): Award-winning playwright, actor, and gay rights activist best known for his 1982 Broadway show *Torch Song Trilogy*. He has appeared in over seventy stage productions as well as numerous films.

Fischer, Maureen (aka Mo B. Dick) (1965–): Actor and drag performer known for her alter ego Mo B. Dick. Fischer has performed in nightclubs as well as appearing on film and television, and was a cofounder of the New York City drag-king cabaret Club Casanova.

Frank, Barney (1940–): Democratic Congress member from Massachusetts who has long been an outspoken supporter of progressive causes. Frank became the first out member of Congress in 1987.

Fremont, Helen (1957–): Out lesbian writer whose 1999 memoir *After Long Silence* tells of her experience being raised Roman Catholic only to discover later that her parents were actually Jewish Holocaust survivors.

Galati, Frank (1943–): Out gay Tony Award-winning playwright and director of such Broadway shows as *The Grapes of Wrath* and *Ragtime*. Galati recently adapted and directed *A Long Gay Book*, a chamber musical based on the writings of Gertrude Stein.

Galindo, Rudy (1969–): Award-winning, openly gay, HIV-positive figure skater who went professional in 1996. He co-wrote *Icebreaker: the Autobiography of Rudy Galindo* with Eric Marcus in 1997 and has recently served as spokesperson for the American Foundation for AIDS Research (amfAR).

Garden, Nancy (1938–): Editor, writing teacher, and acclaimed author of the 1982 young adult classic *Annie on My Mind*. The openly lesbian Garden has written about 30 books, many of which are for children or young adults, and in 2003 received an award for lifetime achievement in writing for teens, from the Adult Library Services Association of the American Library Association.

Garofalo, Janeane (1964–): Cutting-edge, politically aware comedian, actor, and writer who has performed stand-up comedy throughout the U.S. and appeared in numerous films. Garofalo has been outspoken on progressive issues including gay rights and the war in Iraq.

Garry, Joan: Gay activist and the executive director of the Gay and Lesbian Alliance Against Defamation (GLAAD), which strives to establish fair, inclusive, and accurate portrayals of the GLBT community in the media.

George, Boy (George O'Dowd) (1961–): British singer and former vocalist for '80s pop band Culture Club. Known in previous decades for his wildly flamboyant persona, George has emerged as of late as a DJ and performer in the musical *Taboo*.

Gephardt, Chrissy (1973–): Out lesbian daughter of Democratic presidential candidate and U.S. Representative Dick Gephardt. Before beginning to campaign full-time for her father, Gephardt was a social worker with abused and mentally ill women.

Gielgud, Sir John (1904–2000): British award-winning actor and stage director who was considered one of the finest actors of the twentieth century. Though he was reluctant to discuss his private life, Gielgud was out as a gay man and publicly supported gay rights.

Gide, Andre (1869–1951): French writer who authored more than sixty works, beginning with the anonymous 1891 *Les Cahiers d'André Walter (The Notebooks of André Walter)*. Though married to a woman, Gide was aware of his homosexuality from early on in life, as detailed in his 1921 autobiography *Si le grain ne meurt (If It Die)*.

Ginsberg, Allen (1926–1997): Gay American poet of the Beat Generation. Ginsberg's first book, *Howl and Other Poems* (1956), with its homoerotic content, was seized by customs officials and police, though obscenity charges were later dropped; he later won the American Book Award for *The Fall of America* (1974).

Giove, Missy (1975–): Openly lesbian professional mountain bike racer who has won a World Championship and two World Cup overall titles.

Glick, Deborah: Democratic Assembly member from New York City who became the first openly lesbian member of the New York State legislature in 1990. Glick has introduced, and continues to support, gay rights and women's rights legislation.

Goldstein, Richard: Executive editor of the *Village Voice* and author of *The Attack Queers: Liberal Society and the Gay Right* (2002), along with several other books. He won the 2001 GLAAD columnist of the year award.

Gollance, Richard (1950–): Out gay television writer and producer whose credits include *Beverly Hills 90210, Falcon Crest,* and *Knots Landing.*

Gomez, Jewelle (1948–): Writer and activist whose numerous works explore her multiple identities—black, feminist, lesbian—and have won several awards. Her books include the essay collection *Forty-Three Septembers* (1993), Lammy-winning novel *The Gilda Stories* (1991), and poetry collection *Flamingoes and Bears* (1986). Gomez is the director of the Cultural Equity Grants Program at the San Francisco Arts Commission.

Gomez, Marga: Out lesbian stand-up comedian who has performed several one-woman shows and appeared on numerous television shows and in film. She tours extensively and is profiled in the 2003 documentary film on comedy *Laughing Matters.*

Gooch, Brad: Writer and educator. Gooch is the out gay author of three novels, as well as nonfiction titles such as *Finding the Boyfriend Within* (1999). He contributes to several publications and teaches English at William Paterson University in N.J.

Gould, Jason (1966–): Openly gay actor, writer, and director. Gould costarred with his mother, Barbra Streisand, in 1991's *The Prince of Tides;* his father, Elliot Gould, appeared in Jason's short queer film *Inside Out,* part of the short-movie collection *Boys Life 3* (2000).

Grahn, Judy (1940–): Acclaimed writer, poet, editor, and activist who was a founder of A Woman's Place, the first women's bookstore in America. Grahn is the author of the 1984 nonfiction book *Another Mother Tongue: Gay Words, Gay*

Worlds along with several volumes of poetry including 1969's *The Common Woman.*

Grier, Barbara (1933–): Editor, writer, and cofounder of Naiad Press, award-winning publisher of lesbian-themed books. Grier worked for *The Ladder,* the magazine of the Daughters of Bilitis, in the 1960s, and is the author of *The Original Coming Out Stories,* a 1989 memoir.

Griffin, Pat: Writer and educator. Griffin is a professor at the University of Massachusetts and author of *Strong Women, Deep Closets: Lesbians and Homophobia in Sports* (1998).

Greenberg, Rabbi Steve: Openly gay Orthodox rabbi who appeared in the 2001 documentary on gay and lesbian Orthodox Jews *Trembling Before G-d.*

Hacker, Marilyn (1942–): Acclaimed lesbian poet who has published numerous collections of her work and directs the graduate creative writing program at the City College of New York. Hacker has received many honors, including an American Book Award for her 1974 collection *Presentation Piece.*

Hall, Radclyffe (Marguerite Antonia Radclyffe-Hall) (1880–1943): Author of *The Well of Loneliness* (published in 1928 and still in print), possibly the best-known and most important lesbian novel of the twentieth century. Hall, who preferred to be called "John," and her partner Lady Una Troubridge were well known in the lesbian circles of their day.

Hampton, Mabel (1902–1989): Entertainer, activist, cofounder of the Lesbian Herstory Archives, and a key figure in the black lesbian community that flourished in the 1960s' Bronx. Hampton maintained a forty-year relationship with her partner Lillian Foster, and appeared in the films *Silent Pioneers* (1984) and *Before Stonewall* (1985).

Haring, Keith (1958–1990): Gay artist whose trademark style entailed graffiti-like bold outlines of figures and objects both homoerotic and humanist. Haring gained popularity in the 1980s and in 1986 opened his Pop Shop, which sold art pieces at reasonable prices, in N.Y.C. His later works before his untimely death of AIDS fostered awareness about HIV and gay rights issues.

Harris, E. Lynn (1955–): Openly gay best-selling author of several novels, including *And This Too Shall Pass* (1996), *If This World Were Mine* (1997), and *Abide With Me* (1999). Harris has won the Blackboard Novel of the Year award three times, along with a James Baldwin Award for Literary Excellence and several NAACP Image Award nominations.

Hartley, Nina (1959–): Actor who has starred in countless pornographic films and sex-educational videos. Hartley describes herself as a "heterosexual butch dyke" or bisexual, appeared in the lesbian-produced sex film *Suburban Dykes* (1991), and writes an advice column for the lesbian magazine *On Our Backs*.

Helminiak, Daniel A.: Writer and theologian who was a priest in the Roman Catholic Church for twenty-eight years. Helminiak is the author of *What the Bible Really Says About Homosexuality* (2000) and holds a Ph.D. in educational psychology.

Hemphill, Essex (1957–1995): Writer, poet, performance artist, and activist who was a major part of the black gay movement in America. He was a recipient of a 1986 fellowship from the National Endowment for the Arts (NEA) and published numerous books, including *Earth Life* (1985) and *Conditions* (1986) along with several anthologies.

Herman, Jerry (1933–): Openly gay and HIV-positive composer and lyricist for American musical theater. Among his major successes are *Hello Dolly!* (1964) and *Mame* (1966), for which he won a Grammy. With Marilyn Stasio, Herman published a memoir entitled *Showtune* in 1996.

Hoffman, Tyler: Out former pro baseball umpire. Since leaving the baseball world after five years as a professional, Hoffman worked as a financial adviser and started his own "personal effectiveness company" called SportsMind Solutions.

Holleran, Andrew (1943?–): Celebrated writer known for his extraordinary prose styling and gay-themed fiction. Holleran was a member of the Violet Quill Club, a hugely influential group of gay male writers in the 1980s, and is the author of *Dancer from the Dance* (1978) and the 1988 essay collection *Ground Zero*.

Hollibaugh, Amber: Activist, writer, filmmaker, and self-described lesbian sex radical. Hollibaugh is the author of acclaimed essay collection *My Dangerous Desires: A Queer Girl Dreaming Her Way Home* (2000).

Hughes, Holly (1955–): Lesbian feminist performance artist and playwright who has won two OBIE Awards and creates queer-themed works, such as *Well of Horniness* (1983) and *Clit Notes* (1990), intended to spark controversy. Hughes was one of the infamous "NEA Four" whose National Endowment for the Arts grant was revoked in 1990, but later reinstated.

Ian, Janis (1951–): Out lesbian singer-songwriter best known for her 1970s song "At Seventeen," which won her two Grammy awards. Ian has recorded several successful albums and runs the Pearl Foundation, an organization that raises funds for college scholarships.

Jay, Karla (1947–): Writer, activist, scholar, and pioneer in the field of lesbian and gay studies. Jay has published numerous books, including *The Amazon and the Page: Natalie Clifford Barney and Renée Vivien* (1988) and a 1999 memoir, *Tales of the Lavender Menace,* and has taught English at Pace University for twenty-five years.

James, Andrea: Transgender and consumer activist who cofounded and co-owns Deep Stealth Productions, a film and television company that works toward accurate and positive media portrayals of transgender people. James is also the creator of informative websites that provide personal advice and other free content for the transgender community.

Jennings, Kevin: Founder and executive director of the Gay, Lesbian, and Straight Education Network (GLSN) as well as an out educator and writer. His books include *Becoming Visible: A Reader in Gay and Lesbian History for High School and College Students* and *One Teacher in Ten: Gay and Lesbian Educators Tell Their Stories* (both published in 1994).

John, Sir Elton (Reginald Kenneth Dwight) (1947–): Out and hugely successful British musician who has had a Top Forty single every year from 1970 to 1996. In 1992 John established the Elton John AIDS Foundation, pledging to donate all his royalties to AIDS research.

Jolie, Angelina (1975–): Openly bisexual film actor who has portrayed queer characters in some of her movies, including *Foxfire* (1996) and *Gia* (1998); she won an Oscar for her performance in *Girl, Interrupted* (1999). As of late, she is also known for her role as a goodwill ambassador with the United Nations High Commissioner for Refugees (UNHCR).

Jones, Cleve (1954–): Longtime gay rights activist and founder of the NAMES Project AIDS Memorial Quilt in 1987, which now operates forty-nine chapters. Jones' memoir *Stitching a Revolution: The Making of an Activist* was published in 2000.

Kameny, Frank (1925–): Astronomer, writer, and pioneering activist who cofounded the Mattachine Society, the first U.S. gay rights organization, and was instrumental in the formation of other gay rights organizations. Kameny has fought tirelessly for myriad aspects of gay rights, and in 1971 was the first openly gay person to run for Congress.

Katz, Jonathan Ned (1938–): Historian, activist, scholar, and author of numerous seminal works on history and homophobia, including *Gay American History* (1976) and *The Invention of Heterosexuality* (1995). Katz received the Publishing Triangle's Bill Whitehead Award for Lifetime Achievement in Lesbian and Gay Literature in 1995.

Kirby, Michael: Openly gay Australia High Court judge. Appointed in 1996, Kirby has held numerous international positions, favors law reform, and is regarded as a champion of human rights.

Kopay, David (1942–): Football player who was one of the first professional athletes to out himself. He was running back for the San Francisco 49ers, the Green Bay Packers, and several other teams. His autobiography, *The David Kopay Story: An Extraordinary Self-Revelation* (written with Perry Deane Young) was published in 1977.

Kramer, Larry (1935–): Openly gay, HIV-positive writer, and America's best-known AIDS activist. Kramer was a cofounder of ACT UP and Gay Men's Health Crisis (GMHC) and has been referred to as "the angriest gay man in the world" for his confrontational tactics. He is the author of 1978's *Faggots* and the 1989 memoir *Reports from the Holocaust: The Making of an AIDS Activist.*

lang, k. d. (Katherine Dawn Lang) (1962–): Canadian singer who began her career by performing country music and later developed a jazz-influenced style. She officially came out—though whether she had actually ever been "in" is questionable—in a 1992 *Advocate* cover story, and has a large following both lesbian and mainstream.

Langley, Liz: Freelance writer who contributes to numerous alternative news sources, including Alternet.org and the *Orlando Weekly*. Her first book *Pop Tart*—a collection of her columns—was published in 2000.

Lavner, Lynn: Lesbian comedian and musician who is billed as "America's most politically incorrect entertainer." She has performed throughout the U.S. and internationally at diverse events including GLBT pride celebrations.

Lebowitz, Fran (1950–): Widely quoted writer and humorist who is known for her satirical wit. She is the author of *Metropolitan Life* (1978) and *Social Studies* (1981) and has made frequent television appearances.

Leduc, Mark: Canadian boxer who outed himself in a 1994 television documentary, *For the Love of the Game*. Now retired, Leduc possesses a silver medal from the 1986 Olympics at Barcelona, Spain.

Lee, Christopher: Filmmaker, director, and producer whose films include the groundbreaking 1998 female-to-male transsexual pornographic film *Alley of the Tranny Boys*. Lee is the cofounder and codirector of San Francisco-based transgender film festival Tranny Fest.

Lemon, Brendan: Writer and editor. Lemon is a former cultural editor for *The New Yorker* and current editor-in-chief of *Out Magazine*. He is the author of a novel, *Last Night* (2002).

Levin, Jenifer: Lesbian writer who has been described as a "female Paul Monette." Her novels include *Water Dancer* (1982) and *The Sea of Light* (1993). She has also published a short story collection and compiled *Best Lesbian Erotica 1998*.

Liberace (Wladziu Valentino Liberace) (1919–1987): Popular pianist known for his campy performances, outrageously flamboyant costumes, and low-brow interpretations of classical music. Though he was never formally out as gay, Liberace's homosexuality was a given to most people.

Lobel, Kerry: Social justice activist who was the Executive Director of the National Gay and Lesbian Task Force (NGLTF) from 1996 to 2000, which doubled its budget and staff under her leadership. Lobel has co-authored and edited several books and is currently the Interim Executive Director of Metropolitan Community Churches.

Lopez, Margarita: Activist, organizer, and New York City's first openly lesbian Puerto Rican member of the City Council, elected in 1997. Among her other accomplishments and honors, Lopez is the recipient of a Fannie Lou Hamer Award for her service to racial and gender equality and founder of the Puerto Rican Initiative to Develop Empowerment (PRIDE).

Lorde, Audre (1934–1992): Writer and activist who wrote extensively about her experiences as a black lesbian feminist. Lorde published seventeen books, including the 1984 essay collection *Sister Outsider*, 1982's *Zami: A New Spelling of My Name*, and *The Marvelous Arithmetics of Distance: Poems 1987–1992* (1993), was New York's poet laureate in 1991, and received an American Book Award for 1989's *A Burst of Light*.

Louganis, Greg (1960–): Athlete who is widely regarded as the world's greatest diver, having won Olympic multiple gold medals and a long string of victories at the U.S. Diving National Championships. Louganis came out as gay and HIV-positive at the 1994 Gay Games IV, and later that year collaborated on an autobiography entitled *Breaking the Surface*.

Loulan, JoAnn: Openly queer psychotherapist who has been nicknamed "the Dr. Ruth of lesbians." She is the author of lesbian-themed books including *The Lesbian Erotic Dance* (1990) and *Lesbian Passion: Loving Ourselves and Each Other* (1987), and has appeared on several television talk shows.

Lowell, Christopher: Home decorator and host of *The Christopher Lowell Show* on the Discovery Channel. The flamboyant Lowell has also authored the home décor books *Christopher Lowell's Seven Layers of Design* (2000) and *If You Can Dream It, You Can Do It!* (2002).

Lyon, Phyllis (1924–): Writer, activist, and sex educator who cofounded the Daughters of Bilitis, the first lesbian organization in America, with her partner Del Martin in 1955. She and Martin co-authored two books on lesbian life—*Lesbian/Woman* (1972), which won an American Library Association Gay Book Award, and *Lesbian Love and Liberation* (1973)—and have greatly influenced the gay/lesbian and feminist movements.

Madonna (1958–): Singer, dancer, and actor who is described as the most successful female singer-songwriter ever. She has flirted with bisexuality and was linked with other queer female celebrities for a time, though many dismissed this as a marketing ploy.

Mallon, Gary (Gerald P. Mallon) (1957–): Openly gay educator, writer, and social worker. Mallon is arguably the country's most prominent gay youth worker. He has published widely on the topic of GLBTQ youth in the child welfare system in books such as *We Don't Exactly Get the Welcome Wagon* (1998); teaches at the Hunter College School of Social Work; and established vital programs for GLBTQ youth at Green Chimneys Children's Services in New York City.

Manford, Jeanne: Cofounder of Parents, Families and Friends of Lesbians and Gays (PFLAG), which she began as a small support group in the early 1970s as part of her public support for her gay son, Morty. PFLAG is now a national nonprofit organization with over 200,000 members and close to 500 affiliates throughout the U.S.

Mailer, Norman (1923–): Prestigious writer who published his first book, *The Naked and the Dead*, in 1948 and has won myriad literary awards since then. He received a National Book Award and Pulitzer Prize for his *The Armies of the Night* (1968), another Pulitzer in 1980 for *The Executioner's Song,* and was a cofounder of the *Village Voice* in 1955.

Maney, Mabel: Writer of lesbian-themed mystery series featuring Nancy Clue, a parody of Nancy Drew, which includes titles *A Ghost in the Closet* (1995) and *The Case Of The Not-So-Nice Nurse* (1996). Maney also writes a detective series featuring Jane Bond, "James' lesbian twin sister."

Marrazzo, Jeanne: Physician, assistant professor of medicine at the University of Washington, and medical director of the Seattle STD/HIV Prevention and Training Center. Dr. Marrazzo is the recipient of numerous awards, including the National Institutes of Health Career Development Award and the Lesbian Health Fund Research Award, and is a fellow of the American College of Physicians.

Marshall, Margaret: Chief Justice of the Massachusetts State Supreme Court since 1999. Justice Marshall wrote the November 2003 decision to allow same-sex marriage in Massachusetts. A native of South Africa who was a leader of the anti-apartheid movement, she is the first woman and first immigrant to serve as Chief Justice.

Martin, Del (Dorothy L.) (1921–): Writer and accomplished activist who cofounded the Daughters of Bilitis in 1955 as well as several other organizations, including the Lesbian Mothers Union (1971) and the Coalition for Justice for Battered Women (1975). In addition to the books she co-wrote with her partner Phyllis Lyon, Martin authored *Battered Wives* (1976), a book about her work against domestic violence.

Maupin, Armistead (1944–): Out writer whose successful book series *Tales of the City* was published from 1976 to 1989. Maupin has also written short stories and plays, adapted the first installment of *Tales* for television, and spoken publicly on gay and lesbian solidarity.

McKellen, Sir Ian (1939–): British actor and activist who has given acclaimed performances in Shakespearean plays, on television, and in films since the 1960s. McKellen came out in 1988, became involved in gay-rights activism, and was the first openly gay man to be knighted, in 1991.

McNeill, John J.: Psychotherapist, theologian, teacher, and writer who founded Dignity—an organization for gay and lesbian Catholics—in 1974. His books include *Taking a Chance On God: Liberating Theology for Gays and Lesbians, Their Lovers, Friends, and Families* (1993) and he received, among many other honors, the 1984 National Human Rights Award.

McQueen, Alexander (1969–): Out British clothing designer who has received numerous awards, including an International Designer of the Year Award in 2003. He plans to open flagship stores in major cities and launch his first fragrance in the near future.

Michael, George (Georgios Kyriacos Panayiotou) (1963–): British pop singer who was a member of the duo Wham! in the 1980s and pursued a solo career after 1986. He has won several awards including two Grammies and two Gay and Lesbian Music Awards (GLAMAs). Michael was forced out of the closet in April 1998 in a Beverly Hills park lavatory incident, and has since been frank and open about his gay identity.

Milk, Harvey (1930–1978): Groundbreaking politician and activist who was elected to the San Francisco Board of Supervisors in 1977, becoming the first openly gay city official and influencing many GLBT activists to come. Before his death the following year at the hand of Dan White, a former city supervisor who opposed gay civil rights, Milk passed the city's first housing and job anti-discrimination ordinance protecting gays and lesbians.

Mizrahi, Isaac (1961–): Out gay fashion designer, writer, and performer who has created haute couture in the past and, more recently, produced a line of inexpensive items for Target stores. He was the subject of the 1995 documentary *Unzipped,* starred in the one-man cabaret show *Les MIZrahi* (2000), and currently hosts his own talk show on the Oxygen Network.

Monette, Paul (1945–1995): Writer, poet, and AIDS activist. Monette's series of books on his lover's struggle with AIDS and on gay life, such as *Borrowed Time: An AIDS Memoir* (1988) and *Becoming a Man: Half a Life Story* (1992), won him critical acclaim and several awards.

Moraga, Cherrie (1952–): Influential activist, writer, and editor whose works explore her identity as a Chicana and a lesbian. With Gloria Anzaldua, she edited the groundbreaking 1981 anthology *This Bridge Called My Back: Writings by Radical Women of Color* and later founded the Kitchen Table: Women of Color Press.

Mullally, Megan (1958–): Out bisexual actor and singer who won an Emmy in 2000 for her portrayal of Karen on the TV sitcom *Will and Grace*. She has garnered several other award nominations, and has appeared in Broadway shows including *Grease* (1994) as well as in other television shows and films.

Musto, Michael: Writer who has long been a columnist for the *Village Voice* in addition to publishing the book *Downtown* in 1986. The openly gay Musto is widely interviewed and makes frequent appearances on television and in comedy shorts.

Nangeroni, Nancy: Transgender activist, writer, and speaker who has produced and hosted a radio show entitled "GenderTalk," for which she won a 2000 GLAAD award. Her articles have been widely published and she has received several other awards. Nangeroni is the Founder of the Boston chapter of the Transsexual Menace, and a design engineer in computers and telecom.

Navratilova, Martina (1956–): Tennis star, activist, and writer. Navratilova was the first major athlete to come out publicly during her sports career (in 1991). She was born in Czechoslovakia but defected to the U.S. in 1975, soon establishing herself as the greatest women's tennis player ever, with 167 single and 164 double titles.

Near, Holly (1949–): Activist and singer/songwriter who was a major influence in the development of the women's music movement. She was out as a lesbian in the 1970s, though she later shied away from labeling her sexuality; her music has long addressed issues of gay rights and feminism as well as pacifism and racism.

Nelson, Mariah Burton (1956–): Athlete who was a college and professional basketball player and began writing about sports in 1980. Nelson is the out lesbian author of five books, including the controversial *The Stronger Women Get, the More Men Love Football* (1995), and she maintains a career as a professional speaker.

Nestle, Joan (1940–): Writer, educator, and pioneer of lesbian culture and activism who cofounded the Lesbian Herstory Archives in New York City. Nestle is the author or editor of numerous books, including *A Restricted Country* (1987) and the important anthology *The Persistent Desire: A Butch-*

Femme Reader (1992); has received numerous awards including four Lammys; and taught English at Queens College for twenty-eight years.

Newton, Esther: Gay and lesbian studies scholar and writer who has published several books, including *Cherry Grove, Fire Island: Sixty Years in America's First Gay and Lesbian Town* (1993) and *Margaret Mead Made Me Gay: Personal Essays, Public Ideas* (2000). Newton has taught anthropology at SUNY Purchase since 1971; she is also the chair of the Lesbian and Gay Studies Program there.

Northrop, Ann: Veteran journalist and activist who is an out lesbian. Formerly a CBS producer, Northrop became an educator and activist around issues of AIDS and gay rights, and has been an outspoken member of ACT UP and Queer Nation.

O'Donnell, Rosie (1962–): Comedian, actor, talk-show host, and activist who came out as a lesbian in 2002, just as she was ending her talk show and returning to the stand-up circuit. O'Donnell has adopted several children and became involved in the recent Florida struggle to permit gay parents to adopt, making efforts to educate her viewers on this subject.

O'Hara, Scott (1961–1998): Openly gay performer, poet, and writer who starred in numerous pornographic films. O'Hara also published the quarterly journal *Steam,* dedicated to discussions about public sex, and a 1997 autobiography entitled *Autopornography.*

O'Hare, Denis (1962–): Openly gay producer and actor who has appeared on episodes of *Law and Order* and in movies including *The Anniversary Party* (2001). He also won a Tony Award for his Broadway performance in *Take Me Out.*

Orner, Eric: Illustrator and writer. Orner is the creator of *The Mostly Unfabulous Social Life of Ethan Green*, a comic strip featuring an openly gay protagonist, that runs in numerous weekly papers and has been collected into several books.

Paglia, Camille (1943–): Writer, educator, and critic whose controversial theories on biological sex, gender, and culture have earned her infamy. She identifies as a "bisexual lesbian," is the author of several best-selling books including *Sexual Personae* (1990), and teaches at the University of the Arts in Pennsylvania.

Palmer, Dr. Martin: Openly gay physician who practices in Anchorage, Alaska, where he is involved in the fight against HIV/AIDS. Palmer is also an English professor at the University of Alaska.

Parmar, Pratibha (1955–): Nairobi-born British filmmaker, photographer, writer, and activist who worked in a feminist publishing collective and was a youth and community worker prior to working in film. Her queer-themed short films include *Flesh and Paper* (1990), *Double the Trouble, Twice the Fun* (1992), and *Wavelengths* (1997). Her works also explore feminist themes and the experiences of women of color.

Perry, Rev. Troy D. (1940–): Founder of the Universal Fellowship of the Metropolitan Community Churches, established in 1968, which serves a lesbian and gay congregation.

Pettit, Sarah (1967–2003): Openly lesbian editor, journalist, and a founder of *Out* magazine who was considered a major force within the gay press. Pettit later became senior editor of the Arts and Entertainment section of *Newsweek*, where she worked until her untimely death of lymphoma.

Pharr, Suzanne: Organizer, activist, and writer who is a founder of the Women's Project in Little Rock, Arkansas, and works toward building a multi-issued movement for social and economic justice. She is the author of *Homophobia: A Weapon of Sexism* (1988) and *In the Time of the Right* (1996).

Picano, Felice (1944–): Out gay writer who was the most prolific member of the Violet Quill Club. He has authored more than twenty books, founded the first gay American press—Sea Horse—in 1977, and won the Ferro-Grumley Award for gay fiction for *Like People in History* (1995).

Pratt, Minnie Bruce (1946–): Writer, educator, and award-winning poet. Pratt has published five books of poetry including *Crime Against Nature* (1998)—for which she received the American Library Association Gay and Lesbian Book Award for Literature—along with the prose collection *S/He* (1995). Pratt has also worked as a grassroots organizer and is a graduate faculty member of The Union Institute and University.

Price, Patrick: Out gay editor and writer. Price is the best-selling author of the gay neo-classics *Husband Hunting Made Easy* (1998) and *Drama Queen* (2001).

Queen, Carol: Openly bisexual writer, speaker, and educator whose books include *Exhibitionism for the Shy* (1995) and *The Leather Daddy and the Femme* (1998). Queen has a doctorate in sexology, contributes to several periodicals, and performs and lectures widely.

Quinn, Christine: Openly lesbian, Democratic City Council member in New York City who has long been a progressive activist and organizer. Elected to the City Council in 1995, Quinn is the former Executive Director of the N.Y.C. Gay and Lesbian Anti-Violence Project (AVP) and remains active in the struggle for gay and lesbian civil rights.

Raphael, Lev: Openly gay writer, book reviewer, and educator. Raphael's work has been widely anthologized and his 1990 short-story collection *Dancing on Tisha B'Av* won a Lammy. He is the author of the Nick Hoffman mystery series along with numerous other novels and nonfiction books, and currently writes a book review column for the *Detroit Free Press*.

Rechy, John (1934–): Celebrated gay writer and playwright who is the recipient of PEN-USA-West's 1997 Lifetime Achievement Award and the William Whitehead Award for Lifetime Achievement, among other honors. His classic, best-selling first novel, *City of Night,* was published in 1967. He has authored numerous other successful works and teaches in the graduate division of the University of Southern California.

Renna, Cathy: News media director of the Gay and Lesbian Alliance Against Defamation (GLAAD) since 2001. Renna, who was a GLAAD volunteer for several years before becoming a staff member, has been at the forefront of lesbian and gay activism both locally and nationally.

Reno: Lesbian comedian and actor who has written and performed in numerous off-Broadway solo shows and on cable television. Reno, whose work often explores progressive politics, has also made several films, including *Reno Finds Her Mom* (1998) and *Rebel Without a Pause* (2002), which was based on her successful stage show.

Reynolds, Margaret: British writer and professor who has authored and edited several lesbian- and feminist-themed books include *Erotica: Women's Writing from Sappho to Margaret Atwood* (1998) and *The Sappho Companion* (2001). She is also the editor of the Vintage Living Texts series of guides to contemporary writers.

Rich, Adrienne (1929–): Acclaimed lesbian-feminist writer and poet whose classic works include the 1974 American Book Award-winning poetry collection *Diving Into the Wreck* and her controversial 1980 essay "Compulsory Heterosexuality and Lesbian Existence." Rich has published more than twenty books, won countless awards and fellowships, and taught in a number of university settings.

Riggs, Marlon (1957–1994): Writer, filmmaker, and activist whose work, such as the award-winning 1989 film *Tongues Untied,* promoted black gay male visibility. Riggs, who also wrote for numerous periodicals, was an outspoken critic of racism among the gay community and homophobia among the African-American community.

Rimbaud, [Jean Nicolas] Arthur (1854–1891): Influential French poet who wrote the masterpieces *The Illuminations* (1872) and *Une Sasion en enfer (A Season in Hell,* 1873). His scandalous and ultimately disastrous relationship with his lover, the poet Paul Verlaine, has been widely documented and analyzed; when their affair ended after a year and a half, Rimbaud abandoned his poetry career.

Ripley, Karen: Lesbian stand-up comedian and a founding member of the improv group Over Our Heads. Ripley has taught improvisation for over twenty years, and is currently an instructor at the Harvey Milk Institute in San Francisco.

Roberts, Shelley (1943–): Writer and comedian, dubbed "the lesbian Erma Bombeck," who wrote the internationally syndicated column *Roberts' Rules* in the 1990s. She published her first book, *What to Do with a Liberated Woman* (1977), while involved with the women's lib movement of the 1970s. Her later popular books include *The Dyke Detector* (1992) and *Roberts' Rules of Lesbian Dating* (1998).

Robinson, V. Gene: The first openly gay, non-celibate Episcopalian bishop. The New Hampshire-based Robinson was *The Advocate's* Person of the Year in 2003 for his mission to open God's church to all marginalized people.

Robson, Ruthann: Out lesbian writer whose published works include novels, the Ferro-Grumley Award-winning short fiction collection *Eye of a Hurricane* (1989), nonfiction books on law issues as they pertain to gays and lesbians, and award-winning poetry collections such as *Masks* (1999). Robson is a law professor at the City University of New York Law School.

Rofes, Eric: Writer, political strategist, and activist. Rofes' books *Reviving the Tribe* (1995) and *Dry Bones Breathe* (1998) discuss the impact of the AIDS crisis on gay culture. He is a professor at Humboldt State University in California and has been the Executive Director of the L.A. Gay and Lesbian Community Services Center.

Rogers, Susan Fox: Writer, editor, and educator whose books explore the importance of sports and the outdoors in the lives of women, particularly lesbians. She is the editor of the anthologies *Sportsdykes* (1994), *Another Wilderness* (1997), and *Women on the Verge* (1999).

Roosevelt, (Anna) Eleanor (1884–1962): Humanitarian legend and beloved former First Lady. Though married to FDR, Roosevelt maintained an intimate relationship with journalist Lorena Hickok. Her work included helping to found UNICEF and establish the Universal Declaration of Human Rights, and her efforts on behalf of poor and oppressed adults and children earned her lasting and widespread admiration.

Royko, Mike (1932–1997): Chicago-based journalist who wrote a syndicated newspaper column that appeared in more than 600 newspapers nationally. Royko won a Pulitzer Prize in 1972, along with several other awards, and published book-length collections of his columns along with Boss, a 1971 unauthorized biography of Richard J. Daley.

Rule, Jane (1931–): Acclaimed author, activist, and educator. Many of her books, essays, and short stories explore lesbian themes and she has long been involved in the battle against censorship. Rule's 1964 novel *Desert of the Heart,* Canada's first lesbian-positive novel, was made into a relatively mainstream 1985 movie.

RuPaul (RuPaul Andre Charles) (1960–): Probably America's best-known drag entertainer. RuPaul has appeared in numerous films both underground and mainstream, recorded several albums, toured extensively, and acted as spokesmodel for MAC cosmetics. His memoir *Letting It All Hang Out* was published in 1995.

Russ, Joanna (1937–): Prolific science-fiction writer who blends traditional elements with lesbian-feminist themes, and who has also published nonfiction books, short stories, and essays. Russ is best known for her Hugo Award-winning novel *The Female Man* (1975), a lesbian utopian classic.

Russo, Vito (1946–1991): Acclaimed writer, activist, and film critic whose groundbreaking book *The Celluloid Closet: Homosexuality in the Movies* was published in 1981 and adapted for film in 1995. Russo was a dedicated media advocate and queer rights and AIDS activist; he helped found GLAAD in 1985, and ACT UP in 1987.

Rustin, Bayard (1910–1987): Openly gay writer and civil rights activist. Rustin was a dedicated nonviolent strategist who served as chief political advisor and speechwriter for Martin Luther King, Jr., and helped organize the 1963 March on Washington. In addition, Rustin helped to form the Congress of Racial Equality in 1942, directed the Committee Against Discrimination in the Armed Forces, and later worked to link the racial and economic justice movement with the gay and lesbian movement.

Saalfield, Catherine [Gund]: Writer, documentary filmmaker, and AIDS activist. Saalfield's works include the full-length documentary *Hallelujah! Ron Athey: A Story of Deliverance* (1998) and short lesbian films such as *Keep Your Laws Off My Body* (1990).

Saliers, Emily (1963–): Openly lesbian singer/songwriter who has been half of Grammy-winning folk-pop duo the Indigo Girls since the mid-1980s. The Girls have released eight studio albums and have a large following both mainstream and lesbian.

Sapphire (Ramona Lofton) (1950–): Out writer, performer, and educator whose work examines issues of race, feminism, and heterosexism. Sapphire is the author of numerous volumes of poems as well as the successful 1996 novel *Push*.

Saraq, Sean: Contributor to Toronto-based gay newspaper *Xtra!*

Savage, Dan: Openly gay writer. His very popular syndicated sex-advice column "Savage Love" is published in the *Village Voice* and numerous other newspapers. Savage has also published books including *Skipping Towards Gomorrah* (2002) and *The Kid* (2002), about adopting a child with his partner.

Schimel, Lawrence (1971–): Out writer and editor who has contributed to and edited numerous anthologies, many gay-themed. Schimel is the author of the short story collection *His Tongue* (2002) and edited the Lammy-winning anthology *PoMoSexuals* (1997, with Carol Queen) as well as *Best Gay Erotica 1997* and *1998.*

Schlesinger, John (1926–2003): Prolific, openly gay British filmmaker and actor who has won numerous English and American awards including Oscars, the Donatello Award, and the British Academy Award. His popular movies include *Midnight Cowboy* (1969), *Sunday Bloody Sunday* (1971), and *The Next Best Thing* (2000), and he was made Commander of the British Empire in 1970.

Scholinski, Dylan (Daphne): Transgender activist, artist, and writer. Scholinski's 1997 memoir *The Last Time I Wore a Dress,* an account of his experience being institutionalized as an adolescent for his (then her) non-traditional gender expression, won a Lammy and widespread critical praise.

Schulman, Sarah (1958–): Writer and activist who cofounded the N.Y. Lesbian and Gay Film Festival in 1987 and the Lesbian Avengers in 1992. Schulman has also worked with ACT UP, is the winner of several awards for her novels such as *After Delores* (1988), and has published articles in count-less mainstream and gay publications.

Scott, D. Travers: Out gay writer and performer whose work has appeared in numerous publications and anthologies. Scott is the author of a novel, *Execution, Texas: 1987* (1997) and editor of the anthologies *Strategic Sex* (1999) and *Best Gay Erotica 2000.*

Shaiman, Marc: Prolific composer-lyricist who won a Grammy in 2003 for the Broadway production of *Hairspray,* as well as an Emmy award for his televi-sion work and five Academy Award nominations for his scores to popular films. Shaiman has also worked on countless Broadway shows and musical albums.

Shalit, Peter: Openly gay Seattle physician who specializes in HIV care. Dr. Shalit is a professor of medicine at the University of Washington, author of

Living Well: The Gay Man's Essential Health Guide (1998), and son of film critic Gene Shalit.

Shaw, Aiden (1966–): British novelist, poet, and actor in gay male porn films who has included accounts of his experiences as a prostitute in his written and performed work. Shaw's published books include *Brutal* (1996) and *Wasted* (2001).

Shilts, Randy (1951–1994): Journalist, writer, and AIDS activist. His groundbreaking books *The Mayor of Castro Street: The Life and Times of Harvey Milk* (1982), *And the Band Played On: Politics, People, and the AIDS Epidemic* (1987), and *Conduct Unbecoming* (1993) have been described as the most influential gay-themed books of the twentieth century.

Signorile, Michelangelo: Journalist, author, and public speaker who is best known for his work on gay politics and culture. He has written for *Out, The Advocate,* the *New York Press* and numerous other publications. His books include *Queer in America: Sex, the Media, and the Closets of Power* (1993) and the best-selling *Life Outside: The Signorile Report on Gay Men* (1995).

Simpson, Mark: British writer who is credited for creating the term "metrosexual" to describe urban, particularly image-conscious men of any sexual orientation. His books include *It's a Queer World* (1999) and *Sex Terror* (2002).

Smith, Barbara (1946–): Writer, editor, and educator who cofounded and runs Kitchen Table: Women of Color Press and explores themes of race, class, and homophobia in her fiction, essays, and articles. Smith is the editor of the groundbreaking anthology *Home Girls* (1983) and has won several awards, including the Anderson Prize Foundation Stonewall Award in 1994.

Smith, Bob: Gay stand-up comedian and author of the bestselling books *Openly Bob* (1997), which won a 1998 Lammy, and *Way To Go Smith* (1999). Smith has written for publications including *The Advocate, OUT,* and the *Los Angeles Times Magazine,* as well as for television shows.

Somerville, Jimmy (1961–): Out singer and composer who was a part of the all-gay British rock group Bronski Beat in the 1980s. Somerville later began the Communards, whose single "For a Friend" was among the first pop songs to address AIDS. He is currently a solo artist.

Sonnabend, Joseph: Physician who has been treating AIDS patients since the disease first manifested itself in New York and has long promoted safer sex practices. Sonnabend, whose theories on the relationship between HIV and AIDS have been controversial, founded both the AIDS Medical Foundation (later AmFAR) and Community Research Initiative (later CRIA).

Sophocles (495 B.C.–405 B.C.): Ancient Greek playwright who wrote more than 120 plays, although only seven have survived; *Oedipus the King* is considered his best work. Also an accomplished actor and an ordained priest, Sophocles was reported to be a lifelong lover of young men.

Spencer-Devlin, Muffin (1953–): Golfer who was the first member of the Ladies Professional Golf Association (LPGA) to come out publicly as a lesbian, in a *Sports Illustrated* profile. Devlin later became a spokesperson for the Human Rights Campaign and participated in several celebrity golf tournaments.

Spong, Jack: Retired Episcopalian bishop of Newark, N.J. and best-selling author of books including *Why Christianity Must Change or Die* (1998). Spong is an advocate for reform of the Christian church and has stirred great controversy with his progressive views.

Sprinkle, Annie (1954–): Openly queer performance artist, writer, and sexologist who is a former porn star and prostitute. Sprinkle has performed in countless films as well as solo shows internationally and has published the books *Post Porn Modernist* (a 1998 autobiography) and *Hardcore from the Heart: The Pleasures, Profits and Politics of Sex in Performance* (2001).

Stein, Gertrude (1874–1946): Groundbreaking avant-garde writer whose best-known works include *Three Lives* (1909), *Tender Buttons* (1914), and *The Autobiography of Alice B. Toklas* (1933, actually Stein's own autobiography). Stein lived with her lifelong partner, Alice B. Toklas, in Paris, where they hosted a legendary salon for artists and writers.

Stewart, Jon (Jon Stewart Liebowitz) (1962–): Actor and comedian who is currently the host of Comedy Central's *The Daily Show*. He is the author of a collection of comic essays, *Naked Pictures of Famous People* (1999).

Sullivan, Andrew (1963–): Openly gay and HIV-positive British writer who was appointed editor at *The New Republic* magazine at a young age. He has published several books, including *Virtually Normal: An Argument About Homosexuality* (1995) and *Love Undetectable: Notes on Friendship, Sex, and Survival* (1998), and contributes regularly to the *New York Times Magazine*, among other publications.

Tatchell, Peter (1952–): Longtime British gay rights and AIDS activist. Tatchell was a co-founder of ACT UP London and OutRage!, a queer British direct action group formed in London in 1990. He is the author of six books, including *AIDS: A Guide to Survival* (1986) and *We Don't Want to March Straight—Masculinity, Queers and the Military* (1995), as well as countless articles.

Taylor, Elizabeth (1932–): Actor and AIDS activist who formed the Elizabeth Taylor AIDS Foundation in 1991 and is the recipient of a 2000 GLAAD Vanguard Award. Taylor starred in seventy films in a five-decade career, winning Academy Awards for her roles in *Butterfield 8* (1960) and *Who's Afraid of Virginia Woolf?* (1966). She retired from film in 2003 to pursue her activism full-time.

Tennant, Neil (1954–): Openly gay British musician who was half of the commercially successful duo The Pet Shop Boys in the 1980s. Tennant came out in the 1990s and continues to work as a singer and producer.

Tomlin, Lily (Mary Jean Tomlin) (1939–): Celebrated comedian and actor who is famous for her characterizations and has received countless awards, including six Emmys and two Tonys, for her Broadway, film, and television performances. Tomlin, who narrated and executive produced the 1996 documentary *The Celluloid Closet,* has long supported gay rights and acknowledged her own lesbianism.

Troubridge, Una (nee Margot Elena Gertrude Taylor) (1887–1963): British sculptor, singer, and translator who had a lifelong relationship with writer Radclyffe Hall. She came up with the title for Hall's *The Well of Loneliness* (1928). Troubridge, who won a scholarship to the Royal College of Art and had her own studio, also worked as a book reviewer for the *Sunday Times.*

Tualo, Esera (1968–): Out gay former NFL player. Tualo retired after seven years playing for teams including the Green Bay Packers to pursue a career singing and acting. He made his network debut in 2003 singing in a commercial for Chili's restaurants.

Tucker, Cole (1953–): Gay HIV-positive actor in pornographic films. Tucker also appeared in the 1998 documentary *Sex/Life in L.A.,* a film about male sexuality.

Turner, Guinevere (1968–): Out lesbian actor and writer who co-wrote, co-produced, and starred in the indie lesbian romance *Go Fish* (1994). She also co-wrote and acted in *American Psycho* (2000) and played small roles in *Dogma* (1999) and *Chasing Amy* (1997).

Tyler, Robin: Veteran lesbian activist, women's music festival organizer, and former stand-up comic. Tyler was an organizer of the Millennium March on Washington, D.C., and helped launch Internet-based gay-rights campaigns StopDrLaura.com and DontAmend.com.

Vaid, Urvashi (1958–): Out Indian-American community organizer, grass-roots activist, attorney, and writer. Vaid, whose books include *Virtual Equality*

(1995) and *Creating Change* (2001, coeditor), was the executive director of the National Gay and Lesbian Task Force's Policy Institute in Washington, D.C. and cofounded the NGLTF's Creating Change conference.

Valladares, Armando: Cuban exile who had been a political prisoner of Fidel Castro in his home country for twenty-two years. The 1986 book *Against All Hope* told his story, and in 1987 President Reagan named him the United States Representative to the United Nations' Human Rights Commission.

Van Sant, Gus (1952–): Out, successful filmmaker whose films include the dark, gay-themed 1991 hit *My Own Private Idaho* as well as *Drugstore Cowboy* (1989), *Psycho* (1998), and the more mainstream *Good Will Hunting* (1997), as well as several experimental short works.

Vidal, Gore (Eugene Luther Vidal) (1925–): Out activist and successful writer whose works have included overtly gay themes and characters since the 1940s. Among his many works are *The City and the Pillar* (1948), described as the first mainstream coming-out novel, the transgender-themed *Myra Breckinridge* (1968), and countless essays.

Vilanch, Bruce (1948–): Openly gay comedian and writer who was featured in the full-length documentary *Get Bruce!* (1999) and is a head writer and star of *Hollywood Squares*. He has written for a number of television shows and films, appeared off-Broadway in *Bruce Vilanch: Almost Famous* (2000), and writes a column for *The Advocate*.

Villarosa, Linda: Openly lesbian former executive editor of *Essence,* a magazine for African-American women, who came out in a 1991 issue of the magazine. She is a freelance writer who contributes to the *New York Times,* and author of *Body & Soul: The Black Women's Guide to Physical Health and Emotional Well-Being* (1994).

Vincent, Norah: Journalist who contributes to the *Los Angeles Times* and *The Advocate* as well as other publications. Controversial for her right-wing views on feminism and affirmative action—she denounces both—Vincent identifies as a libertarian, pro-life lesbian.

Warhol, Andy (Andrew Warhola) (1928–1987): Hugely influential artist who is considered the founder of the pop art movement. Initially successful as a commercial artist, Warhol later became famous for his paintings of iconic American figures and consumer objects, his series of experimental films in the 1960s, and his founding of *inter/VIEW*—later *Interview*—magazine in 1969.

Waters, John (1946–): Out gay filmmaker known for his admirably bad taste and large cult following. His early films, including *Mondo Trasho* (1969), *Pink Flamingos* (1972), and *Female Trouble* (1974), starred infamous drag queen Divine and were made on tiny budgets; Waters's later films have had more crossover appeal.

Weisbach, Rob: Openly gay publisher and editor who established his own imprint—Rob Weisbach Books—at William Morrow and Sons at a young age. He has published books from numerous authors, gay and straight, including Ellen DeGeneres, Jerry Seinfeld, A. M. Homes, and Bob Smith.

Westenhoefer, Suzanne: Comedian and recording artist who has appeared on numerous television shows, including an HBO special, and performs live frequently. Her CDs *Nothing in My Closet but My Clothes* (1999) and *I'm not Cindy Brady* (2000) both won GLAMAs.

Wheatley, Bishop Melvin: United Methodist bishop who served as pastor for thirty-three years in Denver, Colorado before his retirement in 1985. Wheatley is the father of a gay son, an outspoken opponent of the church's antigay and anti-birth control stance, and an Honorary Director of PFLAG.

White, Edmund (1940–): Celebrated writer of contemporary gay literature and nonfiction, including *Nocturnes for the King of Naples* (1978) and *A Boy's Own Story* (1982). White, a member of the Violet Quill Club in the 1980s, was coeditor of the groundbreaking *The Joy of Gay Sex* (1977) and has won numerous writing awards.

White, Rev. Mel: Writer, filmmaker, and Christian minister who came out in 1993 while a dean at Dallas Cathedral of Hope of the Universal Fellowship of Metropolitan Community Churches (UFMCC). His autobiography *Stranger at the Gate: To Be Gay and Christian in America* was published in 1994.

Wilchins, Riki Ann: Transgender activist and writer who cofounded the Transsexual Menace and is the Executive Director of GenderPAC (Gender Public Advocacy Coalition). Wilchins is the author of several books on gender issues and a columnist for *The Advocate*.

Wilde, Oscar (1854–1900): Writer and critic who was as famous for his wit and flamboyance as his literary talent during his early years in Britain, but was later prosecuted and sentenced for his "gross indecency" with other males. Wilde published one novel, *The Picture of Dorian Gray* (1891), and wrote several plays, including 1895's *The Importance of Being Earnest*.

Williams, Karen: Queer comic veteran and the founder, CEO, and president of the International Institute of Humor and Healing Arts (HaHA Institute). Williams has taught Stand-Up Comedy at Cleveland State University and is featured in the 2003 documentary film on comedy *Laughing Matters*.

Wittig, Monique (1935–2003): Openly lesbian, French-born writer and theorist whose 1969 prose poem collection *Les Guerilleres* has become a feminist classic. Wittig published numerous other books in both French and English, and taught at the University of Arizona.

Wockner, Rex (1957–): Journalist who has been writing for the gay press since 1985. His work has appeared in more than 250 gay publications internationally as well as in the mainstream press. He is the creator of "Wockner International News" reports, a world news source for queer papers and magazines archived on the Internet.

Wolfson, Evan (1957–): Lesbian and gay civil rights advocate and activist. Wolfson was a senior staff attorney and director of the Marriage Project at Lambda Legal Defense and Education Fund for over a decade before founding Freedom to Marry, an organization that seeks full marriage rights for same-sex couples.

Woo, Merle (1941–): Lesbian-feminist writer, poet, and educator who has long been a leader in the Freedom Social Party. Woo teaches Women's Studies at San Jose State University, and is a recipient of the 1994 Northern California Lesbian and Gay Historical Society humanitarian award.

Woodson, Jacqueline (1963–): One of the first authors of color to publish queer-themed young adult (YA) fiction, Woodson is the author of *Last Summer with Maizon* (1990) and *From the Notebooks of Melanin Sun* (1995), among other works. She has received numerous awards for her children's and YA books, which also explore issues like child abuse and racism, and has taught in Goddard College's MFA program.

Woolf, Virginia (nee Adeline Virginia Stephen) (1882–1941): English author and leader of the Bloomsbury Group whose experimental works of fiction, including *Mrs. Dalloway* (1925) and *Orlando* (1928), helped establish her as one of the twentieth century's most important writers. Though married to a man, Woolf maintained romantic friendships with women, including a long-term and well-documented relationship with writer Vita Sackville-West.

Young, Perry Deane (1941–): Writer and playwright who has published several nonfiction books, including *Lesbians and Gays and Sports* (1994), and articles and columns in numerous publications such as the *Chapel Hill Herald*.

ACKNOWLEDGMENTS

Thanks to my incredibly supportive mom, Rochelle Shaw, dad, Dimitri (Tom) Theophano, stepdad, Marc Shaw, and grandparents, Esther and Isadore Blaufeld; to my "in-laws," Joe, Joyce, and Stephanie Baumann; to "Aunt Donna" Austin; to several of my wonderful friends both in and outside of the publishing industry: Rachel Bennett, Andrea Chrisman, Michael Denneny, Keith Kahla, Sian Killingsworth, Johanna Lederman, Lawrence Schimel, and Tami Schisel and Laura Hourican; to my fabulous Bergen Street crew: Chris Aguda, Dana Eskelson, Cade Aguda, Alex Fogarty, and Jamie Tatarzcuk; to my mentors in social work (and beyond): Steve Burghardt, S. J. Dodd, Georgianna Glose, and Gary Mallon; to my excellent editor, Gayatri Patnaik, and everyone at Beacon; to George Donahue, whose idea all of this was; and last but absolutely not least, to my soul mate, Shannon Baumann.

INDEX